Wounded in the House of God

With the Audacity to Survive

ViNita Williams Davis

Wounded in the House of God With the Audacity to Survive
Copyright © 2015 by ViNita Williams Davis
Kingdom Builders Publications

All rights reserved. No part of this book may be reproduced or transmitted in any form or by any means without written permission from the author.

Library of Congress Control Number: 2015951280
ISBN 13: 978-0-692-52648-4

All scripture used by King James Version
Songs named by author or recording artist

QUOTES FROM BRAINY QUOTES~ *Audre Lorde, Maya Angelou*

Cover Designer
LoMar Designs
Wilma R Hills

Printed in USA
Go to our website: www.kingdombuilderspublications.com

The names and places in this book have been changed to protect the innocent.

DEDICATION

That I may publish with the voice of thanksgiving, and tell of all thy wondrous works.
Psalms 26:7

To my Mother, the late Helen G. Williams, who never knew the details of my emotional struggles, but because of a mother's compassion and love for her daughter, continued in prayer for me and other sisters that the Lord placed on her heart. I thank and praise God for her always being there for me. She was a nurse by profession, but she was my personal, private, and spiritual nurse who stayed by my side during those hard times and literally nursed me back to life when I did not want to exist. She never pressured me with many questions, just applied the pressure of prayer to stop the hemorrhaging that was trying to destroy my life. For this I am eternally grateful to this Jewel I call "Mother."

ViNita Williams Davis

*A portion of these proceeds will go toward thy college education of my granddaughter Brianna who attends Winthrop University, majoring in Mass Communication

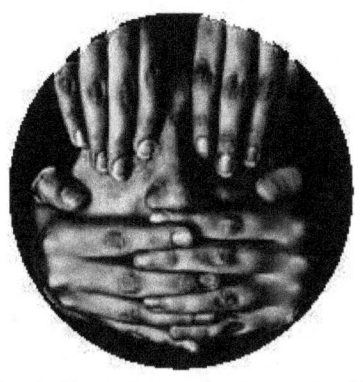

This book is dedicated to my sisters in Christ who have suffered and continue to suffer in silence for years dealing with the inner struggles that come from emotional, physical, and sexual abuse and violations. It is for the sisters who feel alone, shameful and carry guilt because no one believes in you. I bring voice to your pain. To those who couldn't talk with anyone because you felt as though this was your fault, and besides, who would believe you? To those who are filled with shame, guilt, and low self-esteem, and I can go on and on with the after effects.

SCRIPTURE

"Lift your heads, O ye gates, and be ye lift ye everlasting doors; and the King of glory shall come in." Psalm 24:7

Allow me to encourage you by saying that you are not alone; you do not have to suffer in silence any longer. Open your mouth and take a stand against the wiles of the devil that exist in many churches of today. We are sisters in Christ with a charge on our lives to empower other sisters and prevent others from being victimized by people who we trusted.

YOU ARE NOT ALONE

You can and You will Survive.
Trust in God; Have the audacity to believe because silence is no longer an option.
I write for those women who do not speak, for those who do not have a voice because they were so terrified, because we are taught to respect fear more than ourselves. We have been taught that silence would save us, but it will not.

~ Audre Lorde

	Dedication	iii
	Acknowledgments	ix
	In the Words of	xi
	Foreword	xiii
	Prologue	xvii
1	Childhood Memories	18
2	The Escape, Entrapment and Abuse	24
3	The Hope of Salvation	31
4	Silent Frustrations	40
5	Depression & Suicidal Ideation	56
6	The Courage to Break the Silence	59
7	The Letter that Rocked the Foundation	66
8	A New Beginning	72
9	The Cover Up	74
10	The Betrayal of Family and Friends	80
11	Letting Go and Moving Forward	90
12	Recovery: The Wounds and the Scars	95
	Epilogue	98
	Testimony	103
	Review	106
	About the Author	109

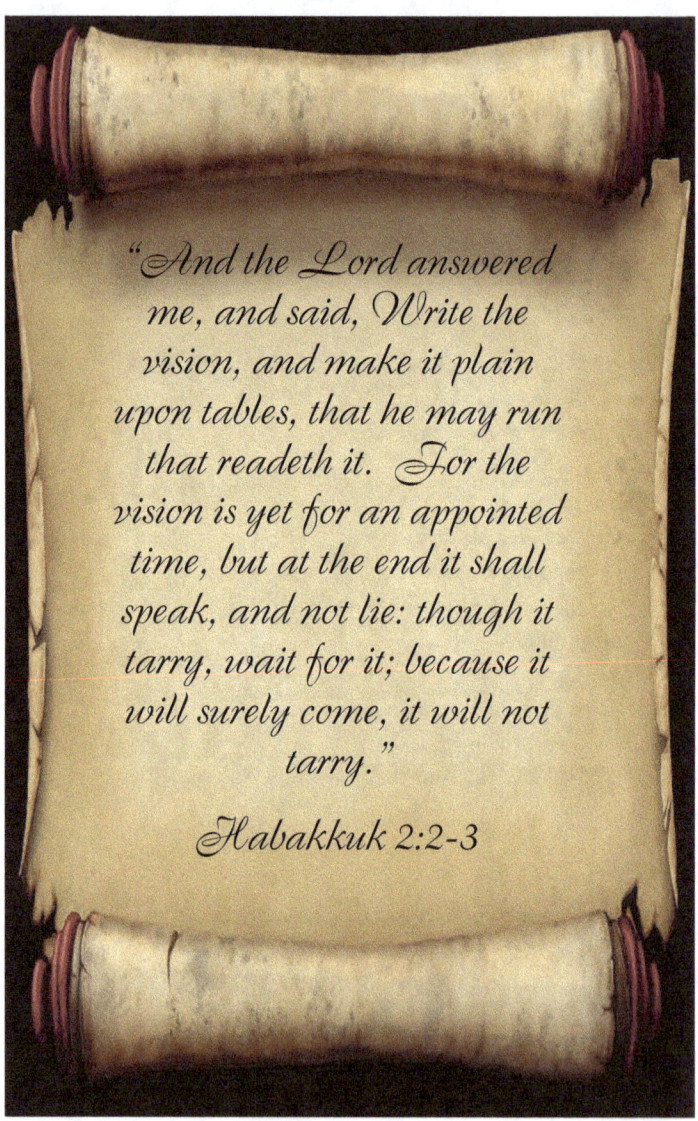

"And the Lord answered me, and said, Write the vision, and make it plain upon tables, that he may run that readeth it. For the vision is yet for an appointed time, but at the end it shall speak, and not lie: though it tarry, wait for it; because it will surely come, it will not tarry."

Habakkuk 2:2-3

ACKNOWLEDGMENTS

I would first like to thank and praise God for giving me the strength and courage to complete this project, and for gracing me with His love and mercy to survive the storms of life. God and God alone brought me through. I am so thankful for the wonderful people the Lord has placed in my path over the last eight years to be a blessing to me.

Reverend Dr. Mary O. Stover, thanks for encouraging me to return to my writing and inspiring me along the way when memories of this journey made it difficult to continue. Your encouraging words gave me the push to continue. In addition, I would like to thank you for doing parts of the editing as well as writing the Foreword.

Thanks to those who read the manuscript and provided me with valuable feedback. Thanks to my cousin Pam for your advice and help with the editing. Thanks to my classmate Kay Spann-Byrd for walking me through this process and answering so many questions I had coming from a new author. To my editor, Wanda Brown who worked so patiently with me to make this book the success that it is.

Special thanks to my Aunt Madelyn who held my hand through this entire process. Thank you for the love and support. You are the big sister I never had. Thank you for being my rock.

I am most thankful to Dr. Roscoe (Bessie) Black who prayed for me and who was with me when I broke my silence. Also, thank you to Elder Jimmie Dias for spiritual counseling, prayers, and support. You both spoke life back into this vessel that was so broken.

VieNita Williams Davis

To my friend, and confidant Ruby Brown, who the Lord sent into my life when so many others turned their backs and walked away, Thank you because you have been by my side and encouraged me to be strong and hold my head up high with great humbleness.

I am especially grateful for my publisher Louise M. Smith, of Kingdom Builders Publications. You have been an inspiration and a great supporter of assisting me by sharing your knowledge and talents of publishing. I thank and praise God for the bond of friendship we have.

To my readers who have been waiting so patiently for the release of this book, I want to thank you for your support and encouraging words once the promotion of this book was released on social media.

Thanks to Wilma Hills for designing the cover for my book. I am pleasantly pleased.

Last, but not least, my children with whom the Lord blessed me. You are who I live for and I thank God for your understanding and staying by my side during those years of turmoil. I am sorry for shutting you out from my pain. I only wanted to protect you the best way that I knew how to at the time, which was in silence. The Lord has so graciously restored my voice that was silent for so many years, and now we can move forward.

IN THE WORDS OF

This inspirational book is a vibrant, provocative, and revealing testimony about one woman's difficult struggle to come to grips with the hidden and prevalent abuse of power in the church, abuse in the home, and in the workplace. Ms. Davis also dealt with sexual harassment on the job, in the church, and in many instances, just experiencing daily life while trying to uphold the banner and standards of being a true Christian.

The widespread abuse of power and the sexual immorality revealed in this book reminds us of the many stories, innuendoes, and rumors all of us have heard concerning men in power and men of God. It is a sad commentary of how power can corrupt even decent men when there is not a "check and balance" system in place to govern their behavior. Ms. Davis tells us how these men tend to "circle their wagons" to try to cover-up wrongdoing or use every obstacle available to them to discourage knowledge about their shocking abuse.

She tells the story of the contempt that is present in the church hierarchy when anyone tries to stand up against the abuses of the men of God. Her story gives a vivid and stunning portrait of what can happen when Christians can rule churches as if the church is their personal fiefdom.

The veil of secrecy and the walls of protection come down in this story and you realize, as you read, the veracity of all Ms. Davis has included in her narrative. The days when church leaders could protect their secrets and threaten members with silencing, excommunication, false accusations, and the like stripped bare. Ms. Davis has managed to tell her story even when the pressure was tremendous and the support of family and friends was questionable. She has persevered and now her story is in print to encourage others to tell their truth. Her story will also serve as a catharsis for those who have experienced the same deceit and immorality in the church.

This book demonstrates the power of the pen and enlightenment to all who read it. Many people will be fortified with the many experiences shared by Ms. Davis over many, many years from the disdain of church leaders and church businesses. It makes you realize and wonder about the many stories still untold by the powerless, the fearful, the weak, and the few who bought into the narrative that these abuses are acceptable because the "leaders" are entitled.

As I read Ms. Davis's story, I could not help but reflect on the more than 40 years I have known her. I already knew about many of her experiences but to read about the whole of her experiences in depth opened my eyes to her struggles in life and the deep emotional pain that she carried for so long. Her bouts with suicidal thoughts and depression gave me a renewed and all-encompassing insight into how she fought to make it through the years.

I always realized her strong and personal commitment to Christianity and I knew she had an abiding love for the church as God's house. Now, however, I understand the complexity of what it took her to hold on as a committed Christian even though she was deeply wounded in the house of God. It has been her challenge and she was mightily tested. She still has emerged standing, virtuous, and victorious. It is a very inspirational story!

Ty R. Washington
Co-worker/Friend
Retired Educator

FOREWORD

When I first met ViNita five years ago, she was busying herself with the tasks before her as the registrar of Central Christian University of South Carolina, in Columbia, SC; but I could tell that behind all of that proficiency was something untamed that needed release. She did an awesome job of maintaining her professionalism.

As our second year continued, we found ourselves not only in the same courses, but also in a similar situation with our vision; we both have Glaucoma, which limits our driving abilities. Sharing that commonality gave us the avenue to become more than just classmates. We were developing a mutual respect for each other because of our faith in the power and authority of the Holy Trinity.

As the summer passed and a new year was upon us, Sister ViNita and I worked hard to get the administrative building at the Central Christian University, where we both work, ready to receive new students. At one point, our bodies insisted that we take a break. Relaxed for a few minutes, I inquired of ViNita, her place of worship by saying, "Where is the church of your worship?" Her reply was strange, initially, to me. I must have reacted because she quickly said, "I am between a place of worship and organization. I call the place I left an organization because I left there completely broken and the hierarchy did not care." We finished the work respectively.

The University opened with me being the instructor of a class, which proved to be advantageous for both of us because ViNita enrolled in that class. Through her questioning during class, I saw that there was an almost frightened spirit locked inside of her. Then she finally asked, "What does one do with information that can hurt a few, but help many?" The Lord guided my answer with, "You pray about it, listen carefully for His answer, and decide courageously what to do with the information."

We did not talk again for another year until we were getting the University ready to open for a new fall season. She asked if we could talk about a decision she had made. She told me her story and that she had kept a journal of experiences as catharsis.

As we continued, her mostly talking, me listening, and the Holy Spirit always guiding, she said she desired to write a memoir. The book would not scold the sinful, nor punish the guilty, but to free those abused by religious leaders, who have used the word of God and their position to manipulate others into their webs of selfishness and faulty, pious behaviors. That untamed spirit evolved into her passionate need to expose the truth of the ungodliness she had endured.

I became quiet as she painfully poured out her soul. She explained that she was so broken that she vacillated between complete submission and suicide. She believed the Bible warns against blasphemy, and she saw suicide as the ultimate expression of rejecting the Christian God. Her faith was still strong to believe that God would make a way out of what appeared to be hopeless.

A few weeks later, we found an opportunity to share again. As ViNita continued to talk, her face writhing with pain, she softened after emptying herself of each horrible event. She informed me that she was writing the book she had previously spoken about, so that other women experiencing these same experiences may know that they are not alone, that they are not dirty and heinous, and that there is forgiveness from those who have suffered and especially from our Omniscient, Omnipotent, and Omnipresent God.

As the book has come to fruition, it breathes a life of its own. It broke the chains of guilt and confusion that held ViNita captive. It released her to seek and trust again; it also encouraged her to study the Bible for herself allowing God to speak to her directly. Moreover, her story dynamically and boldly says to victims, 'Stop blaming yourselves for the evilness of others who impose their own will upon you.'

ViNita has told me many times of the pain she deals when she retells this story, but that she is compelled to finish it because she wants to stop the hurt, and encourage victims to say stop! Therefore, she can go boldly to the throne of grace with the truth.

Today, through the Holy Spirit, she is healing. She hopes to assist others with their process of healing and survival. She also wants to show them that there is good living/life after degradation and abuse. The abused have no reason to be ashamed or feel guilty. They were victimized.

ViNita, I am so grateful for your tenacity, your faith, and your determination to remove destructive barriers and to crumble the walls of lies by faulty, false teachers.

Remember, Satan is the author and creator of fear, but God is the author and finisher of faith, who renews and makes each day new. He is always with us, wants the best for us, and always loves us, *"for we are his workmanship created in Christ Jesus unto good works, which God hath before ordained that we should walk in them." Ephesians 2:10*

I have the utmost respect for ViNita because through

VieNita Williams Davis

her perseverance comes proof of the truth that GOD will never leave or forsake those with whom HE has a personal relationship. She has stood as Elisha stood as he recognized that God had surrounded him with a mountain of chariots of fire before an encompassing Philistine army. GOD is real and so is Hell.

With great respect and humility,

Mary O. Stover, PhD.
Director of Humanities/Director of Alumni Affairs
Central Christian University of South Carolina

PROLOGUE

Come journey with one who was wounded being a molested child, abused in marriage, sexual harassed in both the work place and church. One who has put her life on the line, only to be humiliated for doing what the word of God says, which is to *"Cry aloud, spare not, lift up thy voice like a trumpet, and shew my people their transgression, and the house of Jacob their sins(Isaiah 58:1).* Learn of one who has a heart of gold and in spite of all her rejections and health challenges, has a passion to make others feel appreciated and special. Even in her pain and struggles to survive, she continues to press her way to a higher calling in Christ.

As you turn the pages, you will see how the Lord has kept her through the years, when even she did not want to exist. You will see how she begged and pleaded with the Lord to put her to sleep (death) to alleviate the emotional pain.

This book will empower those who have been abused, physically, emotionally, spiritually and sexually; to give them hope, deliverance and peace that they thought would have never existed in their life. You will understand how the Lord used various songs as well as the Word of God, to help her in this process of healing. You will witness restoration to one who almost gave up and let go, But GOD!

Yes, you can survive all circumstances and obstacles that life throws your way. When the enemy wants you to go away and crawl up under a rock, God will give you the strength and courage to rise again and live a victorious life. You will see how God lifted her up on a higher plane to fly above the clouds. It is then you will understand how someone can have the audacity to survive and declare that,

"I shall not die, but live, and declare the works of the Lord"
Psalm 118:17.

CHILDHOOD MEMORIES
Chapter One

"For I know the thoughts that I think toward you, saith the LORD, thoughts of peace, and not of evil, to give you an expected end."
Jeremiah 29:11

"The Best of My Story"
Georgia Mass Choir

Growing up in Emporia, Kansas, I was the second of six children. My father was self-employed and my mother was a registered nurse. They both believed in strong work ethics, and they passed these ethics to all of my siblings. Mom always had a loving and quiet spirit. She was raised in a Christian home and attending church was her life, even as a child. Her mother, my grandmother who was the matriarch of the family, and whom we affectionately called "Mother," was a woman filled with wisdom and so much love. We often made visits to her home in Carrollton, Georgia. As children, we looked forward to crossing the Lincoln Bridge when entering the city, which was the highlight of the trip. We only knew one route to our grandmother's house and that was from West Broad St. to 57th Street. Once we arrived, we could never leave that street because our grandmother often told us that the devil was around that corner on all the other streets. It was not until the 80's that I realized that Carrollton was a historical city that had a lot to offer from River Street, downtown to Sullivan Beach. My cousins and I often reflect, and laugh because we realized how much we missed during our visits to Carrollton.

Our father was from a small town in Lawrence, Kansas. He had 14 siblings and nine of them were girls. As a child, we visited occasionally. My oldest brother spent many summers there, but as for the country, and me we did not get along at all. My grandparents owned a farm, and they had everything on it I imagined Old McDonald had on his farm. My Grandma, Trudy, died in the early 60's. I don't have many memories of her, only the ones that my Aunt Frances documented in her historical family journal. My grandfather was a preacher as well as a farmer, but he had some hellions for some children, well not all of them.

All of my aunts and uncles migrated to the northeast, while my dad and his oldest brother remained in the west. Because of my father's religious background, and having a grandfather who was an A.M.E. preacher, we attended Crede A.M.E. church that was in walking distance of our home. My parents made sure we went to Sunday school and church every Sunday. If we tried to make an excuse for not wanting to go, we could not go out to play the entire day. Therefore, we became faithful little members and enjoyed it.

While growing up, all of my siblings worked at my father's business. I didn't care too much about working in dry cleaners because of the heat. When my siblings and I reflect on those years, we realize that we were learning a trade and didn't even know it. We see where it kept us off the streets after school and gave us strong work ethics.

As a child, I was happy. I enjoyed the outside. I can recall many mornings when I was up around 8:00 a.m. playing football with the Dowdy brothers who lived two houses down from ours. Their parents would host a Friday or Saturday night party on the weekends in their back yard, and we would dance all night. Tony and James would imitate the late James Brown, they could really dance, and they could do the split just like James Brown. Those parties were nice and wholesome where; children and adults could come together and have fun.

I was molested twice between the ages of 11 and 12, but I did not fully understand what was happening. One incident happened with my neighbor Janice who was two years older than I was and her brother Billy was seven years older than I was. Sexual molestation or performing lewd acts on minors was not the name it was called back in the 60's.

Janice would have me come to her house and make me lie down in her bedroom and allow her oldest brother Billy to try to penetrate me. I don't remember any pain because he never penetrated me, he just rubbed his penis over my private parts until something yellow came out of his penis. When he was finished, they would tell me that I should not tell anyone and then gave me a nickel or dime to keep quite. I would leave and go home as though nothing ever happened. I recall this happening two times in a two-year span of time.

Another occasion was with a much older girl who lived behind me. Myra was a teenager; and I was under the age of 12. We lived in an area that had not been developed on one side of the street. It was all woods with no homes. Her sisters, who were my age, and I played together often. We would play on the side street and make houses with straw, dividing the rooms on the ground. We would make mud cakes and pretend we were baking, and use old empty cans to make furniture. When I wasn't hanging out being a tomboy, I hung out with my playmates, played house, and hand games. One day Myra took me in the woods, pulled her panties down, and made me lick her private part. She gave me a nickel and told me not to tell anyone. I was a young girl and afraid, and did not ask why she wanted me to do this. She like the others directed me not to tell anyone about this; and I did not. I just went home as if nothing ever happened.

I often thought about those incidents and just thought they were the norm. As I grew older, I realized that I had been taken advantage of a minor. I went on in life enjoying my teen years. I ran track and participated on the gymnastic team in both junior high and high school. I often got into fights because I was brown-skinned with long hair. I was not the type to start fights, but I never ran from a fight either. I did not fight like a girl, I would get in the boxing position and fight like a boxer. I was not afraid of anyone; my height gave me the advantage over many of my opponents.

Another fond memory I have is when my neighbor up the street brought their first floor model TV. Phil, my childhood friend had a large family, mainly all girls and their parents named them all with the letters of "P." The movie Wizard of Oz would play on Sunday evenings and it seemed like the entire block would invade Phil's living room and have a great time. As children, we thought they were rich because they owned a color TV.

My first year at Washington Carver High School, I met my boyfriend Mel Bailey. He was a senior and I was a sophomore. I was innocent and naïve' but I liked the fact that a senior wanted me for a girlfriend. During the years we dated, I found him to be unfaithful in our relationship and I began to experience some physical abuse. His parents divorced when he was three and he often expressed to me how he hated his dad for the way he beat his mom. It was not until I graduated that I began to experience some abuse with him choking me or squeezing my arms, but I overlooked that behavior because I thought I was in love.

THE ESCAPE, ENTRAPMENT, AND ABUSE
Chapter Two

"And it came to pass, when they had brought them forth abroad, that he said, Escape for thy life; look not behind thee, neither stay thou in all the plain; escape to the mountain, lest thou be consumed." Genesis 19:17

"Yesterday"
Mary, Mary

After graduating from high school, my desire was to become an airline flight attendant or a fashion model. My dad objected to both ideas. He didn't want me to leave the state. He wanted me to attend his old alma mater, Winfrey University, which was not my choice at all. For one thing, I did not score high on the Scholastic Aptitude Test (SAT). I was never good in math, so I chose a career that would not involve math.

During the time of my courtship with Mel, he was unfaithful in the relationship and displayed some physical abuse. I believe I tried to overlook the subtle signs because I was in love and wanted so badly to escape from my dad's presence because he was so strict.

My dreams and aspiration were dismissed by my dad and

he wouldn't let me pursue the career of my choice. Therefore, I married Mel that is when my troubles began. Things were okay for about four or five months. I got a job at the local hospital in Emporia as a ward clerk. The job provided on the job training for six weeks. After the completion of the training, I applied for a position in the newborn nursery and got it. My staring salary was $1.95 per hour, which wasn't much in the early 70's. I was often beaten by Mel because I would not hand over my check or sign onto loans that I was later forced to do anyway.

As I stated earlier, Mel was unfaithful in our courtship, his unfaithfulness spilled over into our marriage, and then the abuse began. During my pregnancy at six months, Mel was getting ready to go to work at 3:00 pm, I took a steak out the freezer, and he put it back. He said I could not have it for dinner. I then turned the heat up because it was winter and the house was cold. Well he turned the heat back down and told me not to touch it. I went back to the kitchen and took the steak out again. That is when he hit me in my face and I fell to the floor. I got up, ran to the bathroom, and locked the door; He and I saw my lip was bleeding, and this scared him because he thought he had injured the baby. He begged me to come out but I did not. The next day I went to the dentist because he had broken my denture.

After our daughter Ebony was born in February of 73', I took her to visit my grandmother in Georgia. While I was there, I kept having this eerie feeling that Mel had another woman in the house, but I dismissed it and continued to enjoy my visit with my grandmother.

A few weeks after returning home, I was doing my routine cleaning. While sweeping under the bed, I found a powder puff. It was not mine because I didn't use them. I asked Mel about it and he said he did not know where it came from. I had an idea whom it belong to, his girlfriend Harriet, who he was still seeing. Shortly after this incident, Mel went out of town with some friends, so he said, but I found out later that he took his girlfriend with him. When he returned, we got into it and he continued to lie. I called Harriet and confronted her about the trip out of town. She did not deny it. I told her that I also found her powder puff and she asked, "Is that all you found?" She intended to leave it there for me to see.

As time went on, the cheating and abuse progressed. One day I was at work and Mel called me and told me that he had taken all of the furniture out of the house and he was leaving. I called my mom, who was working, and asked her to pick me up after she got off work. When we arrived, all of the furniture was gone; the only thing left in the house was the baby's crib and our clothes. He had taken the furniture, moved it to his mother's house, and moved in with her. I could not understand how a mother could allow her son do that to his wife and child. By this time, I was fed up. I moved to Ann Arbor, Michigan with my aunt. I found a job and my cousin Carol kept the baby for me.

While working in Ann Arbor, I began to notice that I was losing weight. I had gone from 120 to 99 pounds. I felt lots of tiredness and became concerned. I went to the nutrient clinic at the hospital where I worked to see if I could be placed on a diet to help gain weight. The doctors asked many questions about my eating and wanted to know if I had any health problems. I had no known health problems and I was very athletic in track and gymnastic. The doctors asked for a urine sample and the results were positive for diabetes. They asked me not to eat anything after 12 midnight and return the next morning for blood work. The results showed that my sugar level was over 300. The doctors wanted to admit me into the hospital for two weeks to teach me how to give myself injections of insulin. I called my mom to let her know what was going on. She wanted me to come back home so she could help with Ebony. I agreed.

During my time in Ann Arbor, Mel and I began communicating again and talking about getting back together. When I returned home, he had found a house across the street from my parents. We lived there for about two years. Surely, I felt safe being near my parents and was hopeful that he had changed his ways and we could start over. Sad to say, but after a year, I can recall going over to a girlfriend's house with my daughter and his niece to play cards. When we returned, he started accusing me of lying about where I had been. He beat me in front of the children from one room to the next. A couple of months later, I got tired of him staying out all night and mistreating me so I did what he did to me. I plotted with some friends who lived up the street to help me move the furniture to their house because they had an empty room. I called them an hour after he left home and had my friends to move the furniture. They did not need a truck; they carried the furniture by hand. I went across the street to my parents and moved in with them. When he came home at 3 a.m., he was shocked to find the furniture gone. He called the next day wanting to know where his furniture was, but I told him nothing. I stayed with my parents for a couple of months, and he begged me to come back. Let me remind you that I never told my family about the abuse I was going through. They thought that we just could not get along. If they knew what I was going through, my dad and oldest brother would be serving time for killing that man; therefore, I suffered in silence.

Again, thinking he would change, I allowed him to talk me into getting back together. I became pregnant with my son LaRon, and Mel seemed to be upset about the pregnancy, as if he had nothing to do with it. Our son was born 32 weeks premature. He stayed in the hospital in intensive care for two months. We called him the miracle child because he went through so much. After we brought him home, I stopped working to care for him because he was in an out of the hospital with a lung condition. Staying home angered Mel because I was not bringing in an income. The abuse began again. One day he came home from work with a cold, I had cooked a regular dinner, not knowing that he had a cold. I should have cooked something different for him. After feeding the children, I went next door to visit some friends for about 30 minutes just to get out of the house for some fresh air. When I returned, he knocked me down to the floor and pounded my head on the floor. Again, my children witnessed this. The next day I went and placed a warrant for his arrest and the police picked him up. His family got him out of jail. I was afraid to go back home, so I took a few things and went to my parents' house. After things calmed down, I went back home.

In 1978, Mel was offered a job in Gooseneck, Kansas, so we moved there for two years. I came home often because I was homesick. He did not have a problem with that because that gave him an opportunity to do as he pleased. While living in Gooseneck, I met a wonderful friend name Marlene. She took the children and me under her wings and showed us around the area. She became one of my best friends. She did not care too much for Mel because he was so arrogant, and she did not like the way he was mistreating me. She would never interfere in our marriage; she was just there for me when I needed to cry on her shoulders.

After a while, the abuse began again. I was miserable, I hated Gooseneck, and I was beginning to hate Mel. There was a song back in 70's entitled, "It's a thin line between love and hate." I found myself thinking about boiling grits and doing an "Al Green" on him, but I decided to leave. I called my mom and told her to pick me up one morning at 9:30 because I wanted to move back to Emporia. I sent a note by Ebony to give to her teacher telling her that I was withdrawing Ebony from school and moving back to Emporia. Mom arrived on time and we picked Ebony up from school. I had packed up all of our clothes in pillowcases. Again, I moved in with my parents for a while. I went back to the Hospital and was able to get my job back. I also returned to school to further my education as medical office assistance.

After a couple of months, Mel relocated back to Emporia and begged me to come back. This would be the final and last time of our reconciliation.

As I recall the last six months of my marriage, Mel and I were just living together as roommates. We were not involved sexually and there was hardly any conversation between us. He had a new set of friends. The crowd he was hanging out with was different. Some were men, some were women, and even some were gay and bi-sexual friends of his. I felt like a stranger in my own home.

THE HOPE OF SALVATION
Chapter Three

"For there is hope of a tree, if it be cut down, that it will sprout again, and that the tender branch thereof will not cease." Job 14:7

"Where Could I Go"
James B. Coats

The summer of 1980, I joined the Zion Apostolic Church. I chose to be a member of the sister church which was in Chanute, KS. My classmate, Minister Daniel Yandle was pastoring, and this was where my mom and sister attended.

As I stated earlier, Minister Yandle and I were classmates at Carver Washington High School. He was somewhat on the quiet side. I never interacted with him until I became a member of his church in Chanute. He was short in stature, but could deliver a powerful sermon. He was known as "the preaching ambassador" in this organization.

As I continued in my marriage, I learned more about God's Word, and the doctrine. I began counseling with Minister Yandle concerning my marriage. I asked him if

I could leave Mel because I was tired of him running around on me, and disrespecting me. He would always direct me to these verses

SCRIPTURE

1 Corinthians 7:13-16, And the woman which hath an husband that believeth not, and if he be pleased to dwell with her, let her not leave him. (Divorce) For the unbelieving husband is sanctified by the wife, and the unbelieving wife is sanctified by the husband: else were your children unclean; but now are they holy. But if the unbelieving depart, let him depart. A brother or a sister is not under bondage in such cases: but God hath called us to peace. For what knowest thou, O wife, whether thou shalt save thy husband? Or how knowest thou, O man, whether thou shalt save thy wife?

Being a new babe in Christ, I wanted to be obedient to the man of God. Therefore, I continued to do my duties as a wife. The house was always clean and his dinner was always prepared for him. Still, there was not much conversation between us. His friends would often come over, smoke reefer with him, and leave their ashes on the table. I did not complain about their disrespect and habit, I just cleaned the area after they left.

There were times when Mel would allow me to use the car to go to church while he had his girlfriend pick him up and bring him home the next morning. I thank God for Salvation because there were many nights I pondered about being ready to shoot both of them when they drove up the next morning. I did not own a gun, but these were thoughts the enemy would bring to my mind.

During those times when he would be out all night, Minister Yandle and I would talk on the phone. He was still giving me counsel on hanging in there because the Lord was going to turn my situation around and save this man. As time went on with these late night phone counseling, I began to notice that these conversations would take a different turn. I notice that instead of him counseling me, the conversation would be about sex and the length of his penis, which made me feel very uncomfortable. This went on for a while and it really began to bother me.

I spoke with Bishop Turner, who was the Associate Bishop to Bishop Willis concerning these inappropriate conversations with Minister Yandle and requested to be transferred to the headquarters church in Emporia. He granted my request for a transfer. I chose to go to Bishop Turner because Bishop Willis was an elderly man who was entering into his retirement years. These two men were the only bishops in this organization because former members of the Board of Bishops had gone home to be with the Lord.

After Bishop Willis passed in 1987, Bishop Turner was the only Bishop left in this organization. The church constitution states that this organization should be governed by a board of Bishops. For 20 years, Bishop Turner did not ordain any Bishops. He placed an advisory board on staff that acted as a board of Bishops, but was not officially ordained as a Board of Bishops. Bishop Turner was a man who craved power, and wanted to be the only one in charge. The only discipline Minister Yandle received was a rebuke was an insignificant punishment a little slap on the wrist. We all know how the "Good old boy" system works.

Prior to Bishop Turner's self-appointed position as Bishop over this organization he was the pastor in a small city in Colby, KS for approximately 30 years. He eventually groomed his son Terrell to take over that church while he relocated to Emporia headquarters church. I was relieved when I arrived at the headquarters church. I was welcomed by several members who knew me, but I did not personally know them. We bonded as sisters in Christ and our friendship blossomed through the years.

During the last six months of my marriage, we were receiving eviction notices every month because Mel refused to pay rent to his distant aunt up north. I was not working during this time because I was caring for our son who was in and out of the hospital quite often. One day another notice came and I placed it on the table for Mel to see. He came home for lunch, read it, and placed it on the table. He took a short nap and on his way out the door, he said he was not going to pay the rent, which was three months past due. He said I would need to find somewhere to live because he was leaving. I asked him why couldn't we find another place together, and his reply was because he was going his way and I would not be going with him. I was devastated to hear such a blow!

What was I to do? Where was I to go with two children and no job? I did not get upset or even cry. I guess I had cried so many tears throughout our 9 years of marriage; it was not the time to fall out with a nervous breakdown. I had to be strong and make some important and fast decisions. His sister Sheila had a vacant house that she could not move into because of her credit with the electric company. She offered me a room to stay with her if her brother Mel agreed to transfer his lights, which he did. I stayed with my sister-in-law for six months. I applied for low housing and at the same time. I was praying that I would not be assigned to an apartment in the projects. While at work one day, a call came in letting me know an apartment came through in the projects. Of course, it was a disappointment, but I had no other place to go. BUT GOD! The next day I received a call from my mom's friend who had a house for rent. Her son was living there, but she was putting him out because he would not pay the rent. She asked me if I wanted to rent it, and- of course, I said yes. I wanted my children to live in a neighborhood, and I was tired of all the moving that Mel put us through. We eventually divorced after being separated for a year because he had no other grounds for a divorce.

My friend Val knew I was looking for a job. She referred

me to a doctor's office where I became employed as a medical office assistant. My employer was Dr. Blasé, an Internal Medicine doctor. He was a dark skinned man who was about my height. He had a nice smile and appeared to be very professional. After working for Dr. Blasé for about eight months, my nightmare began. Dr. Blasé began to harass me sexually. I was so afraid of him because he had a Jekyll and Hyde mentality. One day he would be professional with the staff and then act like a maniac on other days. I needed a job because I was a single parent struggling trying to raise two children by myself. There were times that he would call me in his office as if he wanted something regarding a patient and then pin me up against the wall and feel on my private parts and kiss me so I would not scream out. So many times, I wanted to scream, but I was afraid. He was cruel and mean. The office would be filled with patients and other employees when he would corner me. This went on for some time and my depression began to overwhelm me.

Finally, one evening after work, I was there alone and he forced himself on me without my consent. I just laid there and cried. Yes, it was rape, but who would believe me? I went home and almost took my life, BUT GOD! I did not return to work the next day. I was through with this madness. Two days later, I went to the local mental health facility and voluntarily admitted myself to the Psychiatric ward because I continued to have suicidal ideations. My family never knew why I had myself admitted. My mom always supported me in my crises. I never shared with her the turmoil's of life that I was having from my failed marriage, church or work experiences. I was hospitalized for a month. I had a great doctor and a team of counselors who helped me to regain my strength. They taught me the survival skills I needed.

While there, I needed to make a decision to file rape charges against Dr. Blasé. I wanted my doctors to help me make the decision, but they would not. They said that I would have to be the one to make the decision and they would support me either way. I thought and prayed about it and decided not to press charges because I knew I could not handle the emotional trauma that would come; it would be like reliving the entire ordeal, and I wasn't strong enough to endure that. I realized his attorney would drag me through the mud, and I could not bear to be humiliated anymore. In addition, the attorney I had confided in, shared the information with his secretary, and she in turn shared it with my co-worker, who informed me. I was devastated and could not trust anyone. Still dealing with depression, I continued in life.

After returning to church, things were okay for a while. A year later, I began spending time with Bishop Turner's son, Terrell, who was constantly trying to get to know me on a more personal level. Terrell was tall and brown skinned. He was very talented in music and could really play the organ well. Terrell approached me when I was very vulnerable and weak. I enjoyed the times we spent together taking day trips to Island Tan Beach. We would take off our shoes, walk on the beach, and enjoy the breeze from the ocean. I showed him where I stayed in Gooseneck. I introduced him to my girlfriend Marlene who lived in Gooseneck, and she thought he was a very nice person, and of course, I did too. A year later, we ended the relationship because he was being called into the ministry and contemplating marriage. After he had been married only three weeks, the harassment began with Terrell begging me for sex. The harassment, continued and I continued to say no.

Bishop Turner's other son Greg was just as bad. He lived up north. He was married with two boys. He had a hobby, photography, and whenever he would come to town, I would hear of his harassment towards other younger sisters. He would ask them to allow him to take photos of them in swimsuits. As the years went on, he would begin to harass me every time he crossed my path. I continued to just brush it off and ignore him. The last time he approached me, he asked me to take a picture in a bikini and again, I said NO!

I came to this church to be saved, but it seemed like I was surrounded by vultures and the brethren saw me as the new naïve kid on the block. There were many who approached me to be more than just a sister; and many of them were married and in the pulpit. I began to experience bouts of depression because I did not want to hurt any ones feelings. As I reflect on those times, I must have been starving for love and acceptance because I did not get it in my marriage. It seemed like I was always a target and I did not know how to speak out against the advances toward me. Therefore, I found myself entangled in friendships with brothers in the church who wanted the friendship to be more than what I was willing to give.

Self-hate began to creep into my spirit, and I was burdened down. Many times, I wanted to end my life because I felt so ashamed for being so naive; not knowing how to stop the advances from the brethren. Entrapment had a strong hold on my life.

Francois Rabelais *once stated "that he placed no hope in his strength, or in his works: but all of his confidence was in God his protector, who never abandons those who have put all their hope and thought in him.*

SILENT FRUSTATIONS
Chapter Four

"Many are the afflictions of the righteous: but the Lord delivereth him out of them all."
Psalms 34:19

"Deliverance Is Available"
Vicki Yohe

After being at Zion Apostolic Church for about a year, and learning of the doctrine that was being taught on certain issues, I began to question the faith that I was now a part of. I realize that we as Christians are taught from the word of God, to "trust in the LORD with all thine heart; and lean not to thine own understanding" Proverbs 3:5.

I was somewhat perplexed by the doctrine that was being taught concerning divorce and remarriage. I could not understand why this church only looked at certain Scriptures and avoided others. I recall writing a letter to the advisory council on giving me Scriptures and explanations for women wearing closed in shoes and not being able to wear a watch or wedding bands. My questions concerning divorce and remarriage did not sit well at all with those who were in authority. I was not convicted about any of the above issues, especially my not being able to remarry.

I believed, because I was not at fault in my marriage ending, that I should be able to remarry if that was my desire. I was emotionally and physically abused. My ex committed adultery and he deserted his family, so why should I have to suffer and be alone the rest of my life?

When I began working in the church under Bishop Turner, he seemed to be cordial, and I respected him. As years passed, I saw him as a father figure. He was someone I could talk to about my depression and my abusive marriage. I had put my trust in him and felt very comfortable in his presence.

I began to research the issues that were controversial at the church. I could not understand why this church only looked at certain Scriptures and avoided others. I wrote Bishop Turner and the advisory council with my concerns, but they ignored my letters. One of my concerns was, why they didn't deal with divorce on an individual bases instead of lumping all divorcees together.

The Founder of this organization, Bishop D.J. Wilson, began this church over 70 years ago. He moved from Cambridge, Ohio with his second wife Sister Mary. I never met him because he died in the 60's, and I joined this church in the early 80's. I've seen pictures of him, and he is mentioned in the history of the church at every Convocation. It has been said that he spoke softly while delivering his sermons. His wife Sister Mary was a little short light-skinned woman who had a beautiful spirit. One of her duties in the church was to tarry with new members to receive the gift of the Holy Ghost. She died in the late 90's. The second marriage of Bishop D. J. Wilson was supposed to be a hush, hush, matter.

It is my understanding that his first wife lived in New York but was not deceased, so why would he make this rule concerning divorce/remarriage. He also bought a fornication spirit with him that was never dealt with; therefore, it still exists in this organization. He was known to be a ladies man in that he was sleeping with sisters in the church. In the 60's, he impregnated a married woman that he had been seeing secretly for 10 years. She, being over-whelmed with guilt, told her husband about the pregnancy, and they both confronted the church in a Bible study. Bishop Wilson stood in the pulpit and told his mistress that she was lying. This is when the church split and several members left and branched out to start new churches.

My girlfriend, Bonnie, shared her experience with me concerning Bishop Wilson's remarrying her two different times because her husband was beating her. When I would bring up Bonnie's situation, Bishop Turner's reply would be, "He does not know why Bishop Wilson married her twice and he was not here to ask him about it." This was just another way to avoid my questions on the subject. Bonnie was not the only person that Bishop Wilson remarried; there were others, but no one wanted to talk about it.

I continued working in the church. I loved planning programs and events; it was my passion. In all of my working, I did not realize that I was neglecting my inner spirit man. I would always go from one project to the next. Working was therapy for me, it kept me from thinking about my current and past hurts.

As the years passed, I had to talk with Bishop Turner to get programs approved. I was also still getting counseling from him about my state of depression. When I would leave his office, he would always ask for a hug, and at first, those hugs were innocent.

Years passed and I would continue to question the doctrine of the remarriage issue. Bishop Turner and the advisory council did not like all of my questions. They came up with the protocol that any questions regarding the doctrine of the organization were to be discussed with the local pastor. This was another tactic of avoiding my questions. Unfortunately, Bishop Turner was my local pastor, well by this time; Bishop Turner's hugs went to another level with him touching me inappropriately.

This continued for years, and every time I left his office, I felt like dirt, and my depressions worsened. Now I have the advisory council telling me that I need to speak with my local pastor, Bishop Turner, about any questions I have concerning the subject of remarriage. I thought to myself, "They are throwing me back into the lion's den."

As time went on, I began to see a different side of Bishop Turner. He began to be a dictator to not only the saints, but also to all the pastors in the organization. He did not have compassion as Jesus did to minister to the people. I began to notice how he treated certain people. For instance, he had no compassion for families who's loved ones passed, but were not member. That really bothered me. He would not support the families with his presence, but would send his associate pastors to visit the family and even preach their funerals at other locations.
The leadership was very judgmental, to the point that they had people believing that members of their organization were the only ones going to heaven. If people were a member and left to fellowship with other churches, they were automatically headed to hell.

I began to withdraw from Bishop Turner's presence by not going to his office for church related information and counseling. Talking about pressing your way to church, it was a press for me. Whenever I drove up on the parking lot, my heartbeat increased; I felt like I was having a heart attack and going to pass out. What I was experiencing was panic attacks that made my depression worse.

The more I thought about how Bishop Turner used me, and played over me for his selfish pleasures, the more I hated myself. I hated myself for being so full of fear and shame and not knowing how to stop him. During those times when he was touching me inappropriately, I suffered in silent frustration because I did not want to expose him and, besides, who would believe me. I vowed to take this to my grave before I would hurt my church family whom I loved dearly.

I met Elder Ballard and his family on a personal level in 2001. Elder Ballard was the pastor over one of the sister church, located in Newton, KS. He and his family were members of this organization for 40 years. His congregation was small and so was his church. This building was built in the 1950's and it looked like it. Elder Ballard did the best that he could with the up keep of the building, but it really needed to be torn down. However, this did not stop the Spirit from moving in the church. The times that I would visit, I thought the floor was going to cave in because we, the saints would be shouting and praising God so hard. I enjoyed those times that I went to Newton on third Sunday fellowship.

Elder Ballard and his wife, Sister Essie had about seven children. As little children, they were taught the love of music from their parents. Whenever they would visit Emporia to participate on auxiliary programs, Elder

Ballard would have them line up on the front row like little soldiers. When it was time to sing, they could produce such an awesome harmony. It was evident they had many rehearsals. It would amuse me when Elder Ballard would be directing them with his director's stick.

There were times I thought that Elder Ballard was mean and too strict with his family. As years passed, I saw a loving husband and father who loved his family dearly. He was only doing what the Bible instructs us do, "Train up a child in the way he should go: and when he is old, he will not depart from it." Proverbs 22:6

Elder Ballard realized that the condition of the church building was beyond repair. He informed Bishop Turner of his plans to purchase a piece of land and asked him to come up to look at it. From my understanding, Bishop Turner had some concerns about the location of the land, but he did not say that Elder Ballard could not build on the land.

Elder Ballard began his building fund campaign, which was quite a struggle because of his small congregation. In the past, this organization would give assistance to churches that were being built and/or small churches that were struggling. I could not understand why Bishop Turner did not support the church in Newton. It was as if he had a personal issue against Elder Ballard.

During this time, Zion Apostolic, the headquarters

church, was building a new edifice and the congregation made pledges to pay a certain amount for the building fund. Once the edifice was completed, the Lord laid it upon my heart to begin sending a donation to Elder Ballard's church. They began building the foundation on the edifice. Things were going fine. I continued to send in donations because I was so excited about this project. I wasn't looking for anything in return. In 2001, Elder and Sister Ballard ask me to come to a special service in honor of me. I wasn't sure what kind of program this would be. I asked my friend Gerald, my dad and Steve who was an usher to accompany me, and they did.

Elder Ballard's congregation was about 30 to 45 members. The service was called, "Giving You Your Flowers While You Can Smell Them" They sang songs and gave remarks thanking me for sending donations. At the end of the program, each member gave me a gift. I was overwhelmed with joy. I could not believe this was happening. There were so many gifts that we used two cars back to Emporia.

However, as hard as I worked at the headquarters church, I was never recognized for my labor of love for the service I provided. I didn't allow the enemy to make me feel bad because what I did was unto God and not unto man. I truly believe as the scripture declares, "A man's gift maketh room for him, and bringeth him before great men." Proverbs 18:16. It was my passion to serve in the various capacities in the church.

I met Elder Sinclair and his family through Elder Ballard. The two of them had a brotherly bond. Elder Ballard's children referred to Elder Sinclair as "Uncle Joe." Elder Sinclair was the pastor at the church in Leawood, KS. He was a very kind and respectful, God-fearing man with much wisdom. With my permission, Elder Ballard shared my bouts of depression with Elder Sinclair. He counseled me over the phone for a while, and the focus was trying to get me to feel better and overcome my state of depression. They both gave me Scriptures for encouragement, and to help build my faith, but most of all, they prayed for me and with me. I had the upmost respect for these two pastors. They genuinely cared for my soul and my well-being.

They both had no idea what I was dealing with; I could not begin to utter a word about the sexual harassment that I had endured since coming to this church. I would just deal with my pain even though it was destroying me.

Then in 2001, I began a relationship with Brother Gerald Utsey. Gerald was a widow, and he was 11 years older than I was. I enjoyed the first five years we were together. Later, it became a struggle for me because I was being convicted by the Holy Spirit for being in a relationship with Gerald. He was one man that I loved with all my heart. He, too, was concerned about my wellbeing. Because he was older, I had much respect for him. I stayed in this relationship for a total of eight years because he protected me from the sexual harassment.

Unfortunately, our relationship did not work out. He was struggling with my bouts of depression. He could not understand and I was not willing to explain because until a person experience depression, they will never understand. I was in love with Gerald and he was in love with me. The only thing that we struggled with in this relationship was our beliefs on remarriage and divorce. He believed if he married me while I had a living ex-husband, he would go to hell. I, on the other hand, believed if I continued to fornicate with him, that I would go to hell. Therefore, that became a problem. I took a stand never be used by another man in this lifetime. I was done with men. My focus was to renew my walk with God and to get closer to Him.

I felt so strong about the doctrine that was being taught at Zion Apostolic, that I often asked the pastor along with the advisory council to sit down with me and explain the Scriptures. It was a very controversial subject in the organization. They only looked at certain Scriptures and had their own interpretation of those Scriptures. I would ask about other Scriptures regarding this subject, but they would not address my concerns. They avoided my concerns for years. I was so abused physically, verbally, and mentally. Moreover I'm thinking, why should I have to suffer by not being allowed to remarry? According to the Scriptures, divorce was not an unforgiveable sin, only blasphemy against the Holy Ghost was.

SCRIPTURE

"Wherefore I say unto you, All manner of sin and blasphemy shall be forgiven unto men: but the blasphemy against the Holy Ghost shall not be forgiven unto men." Matthew 12:31.

From 1996 to 2007, I endured a lot of guilt and emotional pain because I was being sexually harassed by several brothers in the church from the pulpit to the back door, and finally with Bishop Turner whom I was emotionally afraid of. For years, he misused his authority by sexual harassing and inappropriately touching me. We never had sex but I was afraid of him and didn't know how to stop the harassment.

As the years went on, this subject seemed to be a thorn in my flesh, but I continued believing that God would change my situation. I became friends with several brothers who started out as platonic friendships, but in the end their motives were the same; they all wanted to be more than friends. They were very subtle in their approach.

Being a single parent, I was always struggling to provide for my family. Several Elders would help me out financially because they said they cared for my children and me and did not want to see me depressed. I learned later nothing was free; there was always a price to pay that I was not willing to pay.

Another brother, named Anthony Dowling, was very helpful to me as far as repairs on my house and car. I took him to be a dear friend, despite of his promiscuous activities with other women on his job and in the church. Eventually he began to push himself on me by feeling on me and I hated it. I would yell at him and try to stand my ground, but he would always over power me. When I broke my silence, Anthony turned his back on me. He never called to check on me, he just disappeared. That was very hurtful, but I guess he was afraid I would call his name for sexual harassment.

During these years, I contemplated suicide several times. Each time the affliction came, I thought about checking in to a mental health facility for help against the demon of suicide. I did not want to hurt my family and I did not want to go to hell for taking my life. I thank and praise God for allowing me to seek help.

On one occasion when I sought help, I ask my counselor to call Bishop Turner to get his approval to be admitted. As I reflect back, why would I need to get his permission, when he was the one driving me to this point? I was filled with so much guilt and shame; I did not want anyone to know I was being admitted. I used my middle name and Bishop Turner's last name. I stayed in the hospital for two weeks, adjusting to new medications and going to group therapy. I began to feel better and eventually I got to the point where I did not want to commit suicide. As a patient, my voice was still silent. I did not share my inner thoughts with anyone. I was just allowing myself to be given a Band-Aid to cover the hurt.

I experienced a lot of inner anger. I thought about all the times that I was sexually harassed by so many brothers and so called men of God. I was angry because they all had wives to go home to, but were telling me that I could not remarry, while they continued to pleasure themselves with me. I was very weak and didn't know how to stop this behavior. Who was going to believe me? People already thought that I had a mental problem. I thank God for keeping me during these troubling times. I had enough sense to seek help.

Dr. Stewart, my primary doctor, suggested that I see a Psychiatrist to get help with depression. He diagnosed me with post-traumatic syndrome after the rape of Dr. Blasé. I had been on medication, off and on, for years, but I knew medicine was not going to fix my problems. I decided to open up and talk to Dr. Stewart, but I didn't tell him everything.

Later I decided to make an appointment with a local mental health clinic. I had my first appointment with Dr. Coshal. We did not talk about anything in particular; he just gave me some samples of antidepressant pills and told me to return in two weeks. I continued to feel depressed. I really wanted to get better; however, in reality I didn't think I would ever get better. I was tired of struggling, tired of being used, just tired of living.

I cried and slept a lot and my appetite was not good. Unfortunately, I began losing the little weight I had and noticed that my hair was falling out and things were bad, but I made up my mind that I wanted to get better. I vowed to make an effort to smile and not isolate myself anymore, even though I was still in so much emotional pain.

My friend Michelle and I began to talk more and to hang out together. I would notice how she would complain so much about Bishop Turner. She spoke as if she hated him. She always referred to his nasty hands. This made me wonder if he was touching her inappropriately too. I never asked her why she was so bitter, we just continued to be friends.

On my dad's 80th birthday, I along with my family gave him a birthday party. All of his sisters were able to make it to the celebration. As always, when I plan celebrations, I am passionate about it, but once it's over, I crash back into depression.

My Dad was pleased with the party and with seeing all of his siblings. I made myself get a lot of rest once everyone left. Even though I slowed down to rest, I found myself sinking again into a state of depression. I was hurt because my oldest brother did not attend the party. We were not speaking because of his wife who had a run in with Aunt Frances at the 2006 Family Reunion. He was holding me responsible, and I had nothing to do with what occurred. That really hurt, but I did not hold that against him because he was caught between two people he loved.

There were times when his wife would threaten to slice my throat; she was bipolar and hated the relationship that my brother and I had. I told Bishop Turner about her threats and having to get a restraining order against her, which meant she was not allowed to continue to come to the church. However, he allowed her to come and I was really hurt by that.

I began self-medicating with pain pills, hoping they would take away the emotional pain I was experiencing. I just wanted the pain to go away. This was my way of coping, so I thought, but the more I self-medicated, the pain continued.

I recall the last time Bishop Turner's son Greg harassed me about taking pictures in a bikini. It was November 2006. It was his in-laws 65th wedding anniversary. He approached me in the hallway at the church when I was leaving the restroom. I ignored him and walked away. As I was going back to the program, I was thinking to myself, "you are such a dog and it would be a cold day in hell before I allow you to take a picture of me."

In 2007, I began feeling very numb when I went to church. I was like a zombie. My body was there, but my mind checked out. I had made up my mind that I would never go into Bishop Turner's office again. I was fed up with his behavior. I promised myself I would never allow anyone to ever play over me and use me again.

> *"There is no greater agony than bearing an untold story inside you."*
> *~ Maya Angelou*

ViNita Williams Davis

DEPRESSION & SUICIDAL IDEATION
Chapter Five

"Why art thou cast down, O my soul? and why art thou disquieted within me? Hope thou in God: for I shall yet praise him, who is the health of my countenance, and my God."
Psalms 42:11

"The Potters House"
Tremaine Hawkins

As I struggled through all of the inappropriate behavior coming from men of God and brethren in the church, my depression and self-hate worsened.

Many times, I thought about ending my life. I hated myself because I did not know how to defend myself, and I did not want to hurt people's feelings. Instead, I internalized all of the pain. It seemed as though I was always in a crisis. I worried all the time about providing for my children. There was never enough money to do anything. When I would get a lump sum of money like my tax refund, it would be to bail myself out of loans created to stay caught up. Finances also played a role in my depression and suicidal ideations. I thank God that although I was close, I never really lost my hope. My children needed me and I did not want to hurt my parents and siblings. I wanted to be saved; Hell was not a place I wanted to wake up in. I know I was a disappointment to Satan, because he thought he had me several times.

I recall during a Sunday morning worship service, Bishop Turner really embarrassed me. The announcer usually acknowledge the birthdays of our senior citizens. On this particular Sunday, Brother Henry Yandle was out of town. When his mother's name was not acknowledged, I quickly wrote a note and gave it to Bishop Turner before he began to speak. He read the note and gave me an embarrassing look that was obvious to the entire congregation. In the middle of his sermon, he stopped and said, "Oh by the way, someone sent me a note to tell Sister Yandel happy birthday, happy birthday sister Yandel" and continued with his sermon. I felt so bad for Sister Yandel. Bishop Turner could be so rude and cruel at times. I decided at that point, I was through with him and his staff. They talked to certain people any kind of way and his secretary often yells or just ignores me when she does not want to be bothered.

Shortly after this incident with Bishop Turner, I started thinking about churches that I might want to join because this organization was beginning to drain me, both physically and emotionally. I was so stressed and burden, my weight dropped to 111 pounds and my hair began falling out as I combed it.

Meanwhile, my girlfriend Sandra was not doing well. She was in the hospital battling a kidney disease. Mom and I went to visit her. It saddened my heart to see her suffering. She was one of the first ladies I met when I became employed at Kansas City Community Health Center. As our friendship grew, I began to witness to her about the goodness of the Lord. My church was having a week of special services and I invited her to come to church. On that night, she gave her life to Christ. I will always remember the sermon topic that God used to draw her, "A Troubled Heart." The next day we spoke, she told me how the Lord was doing a spiritual operation on her heart, taking out the old and replacing a new heart. I continued to pray for my friend as she continued to fight for her life. A few weeks later she died. The suffering was over and she was now at peace with Jesus. I was there for her children during this process of grieving. Sandra attended the church in Chanute, KS. Her son, Gerard asked me to give remarks at her funeral and I gladly accepted. This was my first appearance since I left Zion Apostolic Church.

Bishop Turner's wife walked out as I began to give remarks. My mom and many others were proud and pleased with my remarks. The LORD blessed me to speak boldly with clarity and confidence in spite of what people were saying about me.

My girlfriend Connie who attends that church commented to someone, "Does that sound like somebody who has a mental problem?" I gave all the Glory to God who had my back and spoke through me.

THE COURAGE TO BREAK THE SILENCE
Chapter Six

"And David said to Solomon his son, Be strong and of good courage, and do it: fear not, nor be dismayed; for the LORD God, even my God, will be with thee; He will not fail thee, nor forsake thee, until thou hast finished all the work for the service of the house of the LORD."
I Chronicles 28:20

"Encourage Yourself"
Donald Lawrence

In March of 2007, my Aunt Bernice was having a surprise 75th birthday dinner for my Uncle Sonny in Carrollton, GA. I recall being very depressed on the Friday night before leaving for Carrollton.
As I lay there, I cried unto the Lord. I asked Him to put me to sleep (death) because I was so tired of living in this state of depression. I pleaded, begged, and believed that He would grant me my request.

Finally, I fell asleep some time during the night. When I awoke, I was very disappointed that I was still alive. So I thought, "O well, I'll just drive to Carrollton by myself." I collected all of my TD Jakes and Barbara Amos cassette tapes. I can re-call that day so vividly. I cried and prayed all the way to Carrollton while listening to the tapes. The sermons were ministering to my mind and heart. I had to perform CPR on myself, willing my soul back to Christ and surrendering all. The sermon by Bishop Amos was entitled, "God Said Breathe," and that's what I did on my way to Carrollton, GA. I thanked and praised God for that message even though I had listened to that tape repeatedly so many years. God used that message to start the beginning of healing and restoration for my inner man.

I went to the dinner for Uncle Sonny. It was good being in a different environment because it took my mind off my pain. The ride back gave me time to think and pray, and I realized that I needed help as soon as possible.

After returning from my Uncles 75th birthday in Carrollton, I did not go to church the following day. I needed some quiet time to commune with God regarding the steps for membership at Zion Apostolic. Still sad, depressed and wondering why the Lord did not grant my request of putting me to sleep (death), I realized God must have a purpose for me, but what that purpose was, I did not know at the time.

When I awoke on Sunday morning, my mind was made up not to return to Zion Apostolic.
I spent the day listening to the Word on television. I lounged around most of the day trying to stay focused on

positive things while still contemplating leaving this church.

Around 1:00 pm, Elder Sinclair called and was encouraging me with the word of God and telling how the service was truly anointed. His sermon topic was, "It's Time for a Change." I knew it was confirmation on some decisions that I was praying about.

Later the same day, Sister Essie called me from Newton wanting to know if it was okay for Elder Ballard to visit me. I really was in an isolation mode and just wanted to be by myself, but I told them come on. They both arrived around 3:00 pm. We greeted each other with an embrace and Elder Ballard went straight to the restroom to wash his hands while Sister Essie and I talked briefly. When Elder Ballard returned to the living room, he asked if he could pray for me and I said yes. He anointed my forehead with oil and began to pray. As he prayed for about 15 minutes, I began to weep and wail. I cried for at least 30 minutes after he prayed for me. I know the Lord was beginning the process of cleansing me from all the hurt I endured while at Zion Apostolic.

When I stopped crying, the Lord had restored my voice that had been silent for almost three decades. It was then that the Lord gave me the strength and courage to break my silence. I shared with Elder and Sister Ballard the inappropriate touching from Bishop Turner and the sexual harassment from the brethren in the church. I told them about the many suicidal ideations I had because of self-hatred, for not knowing how to stop the harassment. I was ashamed and felt so dirty for allowing this to happen for so many years. Elder Ballard asked if he could share this with Elder Sinclair so that they could pray about this to get some direction from the Lord on how my allegations could be investigated. I agreed to his request. They stayed with me until my son returned home. They did not judge me; they only spoke kind words to encourage me. Once they returned home, they called to check on me. I told them I was fine and in bed getting ready to go to sleep.

On Monday morning, I called the secretary at the church to make an appointment to speak with Bishop Turner. My appointment was scheduled for 3:00 pm. When I drove up on the churchyard, I was very nervous, but I was determine to move forward with my decision to leave Zion Apostolic. The Lord had given me the courage to face Bishop Turner.

When I arrived, his secretary was working in Bishop Turner's office. We met across the hall in the conference room, which had a glass opening on the door that helped alleviate the nervousness that I was experiencing. I told him I was leaving the church because they did not have a ministry for hurting and abused people or those who had mental illness such as depression. I also told him I did not like the way they looked down on people. I was determined not to place blame on anyone because I knew whatever I said would be his next sermon topic.

He asked me about my son who loved the entire membership. He said it would be selfish of me to move him. I told him that I would not move him. He asked about my parents and this decision. I told him that finally it was all about me and no one else mattered. The conversation lasted about ten minutes. As I was leaving, he asked me if I would write him a letter, and I said no because I did not have anything else to say.

When I walked outside to my car, I breathed in the fresh spring that was in the air; I felt so light because that burden was lifted off my shoulders. My next step was to tell my parents which was an even harder step because I knew they would not understand. When I arrived, I asked my mom and sister to come in the room where my dad was sitting. I told them of my decision to leave Zion Apostolic. I wanted them to know firsthand instead of hearing it from others. My dad began asking questions on why I was leaving. Again, I would not place blame on anyone. He asked if someone had done something to me and I said no. My sister Marie asked why I couldn't just transfer to one of the sister churches nearby. I told her that I did not want to be in this organization anymore and that the Lord was beginning to do a new thing in my life, and it could not be done in this organization. My dad began asking me more and more questions. I began to cry because I knew I was hurting my family, and if they knew the real reason, it would hurt them even more.

As I was leaving, my mom walked me to the car to

encourage me to get under a covering and not stop going to church. I assured her that I would be searching for a church to attend. She called me later. I thanked her for being supportive, and she assured me that she would be there for me. I felt so relieved when she told me that. It didn't matter anymore because my Mom gave me her blessings. The yolk and bondage that I have been through was now broken and I felt so FREE.

Ebony came over and I told her what was going on and gave her instructions on what to do in the event that I should die before I find a new church.

Elder Ballard called that evening to say that he and Elder Sinclair had breakfast and Elder Sinclair cried when Elder Ballard shared my story. They had no idea what I was going through. They were counseling me about my depression, but never knew the cause.

As the days passed, I began receiving phone calls from church members. They were concerned because they hadn't seen me at church. Sister Yandle called me to say that my leaving was a mistake. I respectfully told her that I wasn't leaving the Lord, just the organization. Later, Sister Lois called and I explained to her the best that I could without going into details. She was very hurt and she too cried; but I assured her that I would stay in contact.

My girlfriend Melanie told me that her mom Rita wanted to talk with me and wanted to know if she could have my number, I said sure. I met Rita at a birthday party a few years ago. While attending Zion Apostolic, I would always here about Rita Addison. She attended Zion Apostolic as a teenager in the late 50's and she too went through a lot of church hurt from Bishop Wilson, the founder and other brethren at Zion Apostolic. When she called, she shared with me so many hurtful things that she had gone through from the pulpit to the pews. She encouraged me to hold my head up and not look back. I felt so relieved to have someone to talk to who understood my pain. I thank God for sending her into my life at that appointed time.

ViNita Williams Davis

THE LETTER THAT ROCKED THE FOUNDATION
Chapter Seven

"It is the spirit that quickeneth; the flesh profiteth nothing: the words that I speak unto you, they are spirit, and they are life." John 6:63

"I Speak Life"
Donald Lawrence

Minister Tim Allan witnessed to me when I was seeking salvation. He had a passion for winning souls for Christ. He and Minister Yandle did a lot of traveling to local cities and several states ministering to people about the plan of salvation. They were young adults in college during this time. Once Minister Allan completed college, he continued to obtain his Masters and PhD. He then relocated to New Kensington, PA where he is now practicing law as an attorney.

I called Attorney Allan to get advice on how I should handle this situation. He also cried as I told him what I had been going through. He prayed a powerful prayer with me. He advised me that there should be a group of elders assigned to investigate my allegations. I shared this information with Elder Ballard and he made calls to a few pastors to share this information. Elder Ballard asked me to give them time to form a committee and continue to pray.

A few weeks later, I made the decision to write the letter. I informed Attorney Allan, and he asked that I send him a copy.

While waiting for the elders to consult on the sexual harassment allegations in this organization, I decided to write the letter Bishop Turner requested. For the last 20 plus years, this organization has operated on the constitution established in the 60's that called for a Board of Bishops. All of the Bishops had passed away, leaving Turner as the only standing Bishop in this organization. He established an advisory council that consisted of elders from different sister churches within the organization. He gave the impression that no one in the ministerial body was qualified to be ordained as a bishop. Therefore, he remained the only presiding bishop, which left me no choice but to copy my letter to all of the pastors in this organization expressing the degradation I endured from this bishop and other brethren in this organization. He gave the impression that no one in the ministerial body was qualified to be ordained as a bishop. Therefore, he remained the only presiding bishop, leaving me with no other choice than to copy my letter to all of the pastors in this organization expressing the hurt and pain I endured from Bishop Turner and other brethren in this organization.

ViNita Williams Davis

Greetings Bishop Turner,

The purpose of this letter is to inform you of my reasons for leaving Zion Apostolic Church.

As I stated to you in our last conversation, I can no longer attend this church because I have been depressed for over 25 years and on and off antidepressants that never seemed to help me. In addition, I told you that this church does not have a ministry for people with mental illness such as depression, and for that reason, I needed to leave this church to take care of myself both mentally and spiritually. As you recall, our conversation lasted no more than ten minutes, and as I was leaving, you asked me to write you a letter. I said no because I was not in the right frame of mind and I wanted to get out of your presence. Now that I have had time to process my thoughts, the LORD has given me the courage to express to you the real reasons for making this decision, which includes a long history of sexual harassment and abuse by you and other members of the clergy at Zion Apostolic.

1. I have been a member of this church for almost 28 years. When I joined this church I attended the Chanute Assembly from 1981-1983. In 1983, I came to you and explained to you that I wanted a transfer from the Chanute Assembly because of the inappropriate conversations with Elder Yandle when he would counsel me by phone. The inappropriate conversations consisted of Minister Yandle making sexual comments about the size of his penis, which made me feel very uncomfortable. You along with Bishop Willis granted my request. I sincerely hope you discussed and applied some disciplinary action to Minister Yandle.

As I began to serve the Lord at the home church in Emporia, I began to experience some of the same sexual harassment, but at a different level. I did not know how to deal with any of this because it was done so subtly and against my will. As I look back, I see how I was taken advantage of by those who misused their power and position. I saw myself going in and out of seasons of depression because I did not know how to defend myself against this type of behavior coming from those I trusted.

As I continued to try to survive and serve God in the midst of my depression, you came along in 1996 and started in on me with the same inappropriate sexual behaviors. Yes, the first time you touched me, you confessed and apologized for your actions. However, as the years went by, you continued to touch me in the same ways. Yes, I allowed it to continue because I was so afraid and intimidated by you. I was trapped in a situation that I did not know how to get out. I want you to know that you hurt me and destroyed my self-esteem.

I was an active member in the church, and I often had to come to you to for approval for different programs and counseling. I hated coming to your office. Each time I would leave, you asked for a hug, feel on my breast, and kiss my neck. When I would leave your office, I felt like dirt and my depression worsened. It finally came to a point in November 2006 when I made up my mind never to enter your office again. By this time, I was becoming bitter and numb. I continued to come to church, feeling like a zombie. I was hurting emotionally, and feeling so ashamed and guilty for allowing you to play over me and not knowing how to stop it.

On March 9 2007, I was so depressed, I begged the Lord to put me to sleep because I could no longer bear the emotional pain. Well, as you can see, the Lord did not grant my request. I realized He has a purpose for me. That entire weekend I cried out unto the Lord to help me make the decision to leave this church. This was the hardest decision that I have had to make in my life. I felt like I was being forced out of the church that I loved so dearly. I counted the cost and I considered all of the saints because I knew this was going to hurt them. I also knew that if I was to continue to exist in this world, I had to leave this corrupt organization. I was tired in my mind, and my spirit was so broken until I began to experience chest pains and shortness of breath. In three months, I lost 13 lbs. That is when I stepped back and looked at the situation and received my confirmation from the Lord to leave this place.

2. In addition to your unwanted sexual solicitations and behaviors, I was tired of your son, Terrell, harassing me about going to bed with him. I was also tired of your other son, Greg, harassing me about taking a picture in a bikini every time he came in town and crossed my path.

3. I appealed to you and the advisory council on so many occasions, asking that you take a second look at this divorce/remarriage doctrine. No one wanted to sit down with me to discuss this matter. I questioned why Bishop Wilson remarried Sister Bonnie and some others, but your response to me was that he was not here to answer that question. Yet Sister Bonnie is here, and. said he remarried her because of spousal abuse. The last time I appealed to the council, they told me I had to talk to my local pastor. Oh how that grieved me. The council sending me back in the lion's den to be sexually molested.

I began to get more depressed. Here it is, all of these so-called men of God telling me that I cannot remarry, but they continue to pleasure themselves by misusing their authority. This angered me very much. Let me tell you why! I've always wanted to be married so I could have someone to cover and protect me from the vultures in this world. It has been rumored for many years that the men of God at Zion Apostolic used their influence and power to abuse trusting and unsuspecting sisters. Obviously, I can't do anything about what allegedly happen in the 50's and 60's. However, I can do something about my situation, which I hope will have a positive impact upon the future of the body of Christ.

4. I will never attend another church where one man is in total control. You are not held accountable to anyone but God. Where is the Board of Bishops? Have you not appointed a Board of Bishops in compliance with the church constitution because you want to be the headman in charge? Well, if you had a Board of Bishops in place, I could have gone to them with this situation, and not copied this letter to all of the pastors in this organization.

I toiled and prayed about writing this letter. This is not about getting revenge because vengeance is the LORD's and He will repay. I have spoken to other sisters who you have harassed. They are afraid, as I was to confront you, thinking that people will say it was our fault. Remember, Adam said the same thing about Eve. I had the same thoughts, that the blame would be placed on me for allowing this to happen. However, the Lord spoke to me and assured me that none of this was my fault, that these men took advantage of me and misused their authority. No, I do not have any proof, it would be your word against mine, but I do have proof of other things that I will use if I have to.

The Lord has shown me mercy so many times and has taught me to be merciful to others. The only reason I did not go public with this is that it would hurt the BODY OF CHRIST. There are too many sinners out here to be saved. If they keep hearing mess like this on the news and in the paper, they will never come to Christ for fear that they may be violated too. I don't want to cripple your family or my family with this information, but I am making some pastors of this organization aware of these types of behaviors. They can do what they want with this information, which probably is nothing because no one wants to confront or challenge you.

Saints have called me and actually cried on the phone because of my leaving. They don't understand and I can't tell them because I don't want to cripple them. I just want it to STOP! Another generation should not have to continue to go through this immorality in God's church. I am so afraid of this happening to other sisters and their not knowing how to deal with this. You can ask any woman who has been violated, why she did not tell anyone, the two main reasons will be fear and shame.

I am only doing what the WORD says, and that is to "Cry loud and spare not, show my people their transgressions and the house of Jacob their SIN." Isaiah 58: 1. The WORD also says handle church business in the church among you, so here it is, handle it.

I have suffered in silence, for years and could not talk to anyone about this, but God. I said I would take this to my grave and it almost took me out of here. I feel like my life has been shipwrecked by this organization. However, since I have broken my silence, I am receiving counseling to help me get through this episode in my life. I once thought I would never join another church, but I quickly realized that I need a covering with a good under shepherd to guide me, and give an account for my soul.

I have been damaged both emotionally and spiritually, but I am going to be all right. If I can survive this storm, I can make it. I have learned one thing in this organization that I will take with me, and that is, to never be caught behind closed doors with so-called men of God. I won't judge all men of God and lump them all in the same category as you do divorcees. There are some real honest saved men of God.

I pray that God will grant you repentance for all your unjust acts and give you a heart of compassion for the people of God. I pray that the Lord will raise up true and honest men to lead His people to that promised land. I pray and speak VICTORY over this generational curse that dwells in many church organizations, including Zion Apostolic.

Be careful what you ask for. You asked for a letter, and now you have it.

Yours truly,

ViNita Williams Davis

A NEW BEGINNING
Chapter Eight

"My soul thirsteth for God, for the living God: when shall I come and appear before God?"
Psalms 42:2

"Thirsty"
Marvin Sapp

As the lyrics of this song states, I became even thirstier for the Lord. While I waited, I continued to seek the Lord about the church He wanted me to join. The Lord led me to a Pentecostal/Apostolic church that was about 20 minutes from my home. I called to make an appointment with the pastor, Bishop Barry Scott, before Bible study. After talking with him for an hour concerning my brokenness, I believed the Lord wanted me to be planted at this church. I felt very comfortable with Bishop Scott. He assured me that if I ever needed to speak with someone, that he had no problem with me speaking with his wife or both of them. That certainly calmed my nerves down to know that I was given this option to speak with the First Lady. Bishop Scott introduced me to the congregation before Bible study, and I was welcomed by the saints with loving embrace.

While being there at Pentecostal/Apostolic Christian Ministries, I promised the Lord that I would not get involved with any church work. I was broken and I wanted to regain my strength and just sit at the feet of the man of God and be fed the living Word of God.

As months passed, I felt a little better because of my new environment. I was hungry for the Word of God like never before. I praise God for waiting on me. I felt as if I never had the chance to be saved at Zion Apostolic because so many distractions were vexing my soul; hindering my walk with the Lord. Now, I feel restored.

Because of my thirst and hunger for the living Word, I enrolled in R. A. Bellinger Bible College. It was a blessing to meet new friends and to understand the Scriptures. I was appointed team captain with a study group and president of the Student Government. I was so excited about fulfilling my dream of going to college.

While at R.A. Bellinger Bible College, my major was Women's Ministries. My goal wasn't to preach, but to minister to hurting and abused women. One of my assignments was to visit Greenware Detention Center on Wednesdays to counsel with women inmates. This assignment was very helpful in my personal growth and healing process. I did not judge why they were there, I was there for the sole purpose of ministering in prayer and counseling to sisters troubled. I thank God for the experience to witness to the inmates. In addition, it allowed me to get away from the emotions of my own sadness.

ViNita Williams Davis

THE COVER UP
Chapter Nine

"No weapon that is formed against thee shall proper; and every tongue that shall rise against thee in judgment thou shalt condemn. This is the heritage of the servants of the LORD, and their righteousness is for me, saith the LORD." Isaiah 54:17

"No Weapon Form"
Fred Hammond

Once the letter marked CONFIDENTIAL was received by the pastors, it vastly became public knowledge. The pastors who received the letter were very shocked. Most of them received the letter on a Friday; however, Elder Cunningham who is the pastor of the church in McPherson, KS did not get his letter until Sunday morning. He called me Sunday night to say he read the letter and was so sorry to hear about what I had gone through. He told me, "The church should be a safe haven for the saints." He made an offered to transfer to his church, but I declined by saying I found a new church. He ended by saying he would call Bishop Turner the next day discussing this letter. I thanked him for calling and we ended the call.

This is the memo that was sent from Elder Fred Winfrey, who pastored the church in Overland Park, KS. He was appointed chair of the investigating committee. This memo was sent to the elders who received my letter.

> *Praise the LORD,*
>
> *By now, you should have received a letter marked CONFIDENTIAL. We are not taking the content of this letter lightly. We are working to resolve this matter.*
>
> *Please do not share the content of this letter with anyone else. Sharing information contained in this letter with others before we resolve this matter, will affect all of us in a negative way, and will destroy the faith of many. It is our duty to protect the people of God.*
>
> *You will receive additional information soon.*
> *Thanks for your prayers.*
>
> *Elder F. Winfrey*
> *Chairman of the Advisory Council*

On this particular Friday at 3:45 pm, I received a call from Bishop Turner while talking with my friend Betty on the phone. I did not answer. The Holy Spirit told me to close my front door. As I approached the door, a horn blew. A light silver SUV was in my driveway. Someone from the vehicle said praise the Lord. Because I didn't recognize the car, I didn't recognize the voice. It could have been someone who received the letter I wrote. As I approached the car, I realized it was Bishop

Turner. If I had known it was Turner, I would not have come across my threshold. He asked me to hold on, wanting to tell me something. He told me he was sorry and wished I'd run him over with an 18-wheeler instead of exposing him like I did to all of the pastors. I just walked back into my house and closed the door. Two days later, he repeated his anonymous car bit coming to my home knowing I would not recognize these vehicles. He was in front of my house calling on his cell phone begging me to pick up the phone. He realized finally I wasn't going to answer my phone, so he drove off.

On Tuesday, Elder Cunningham called asking for a meeting to discuss the allegations in the letter written. I very hesitantly said yes. We agreed to meet at a public restaurant the next day.

Elder Snipes from the church in Pembroke Pines, FL called to let me know that an Elders Council had been called to investigate the allegations against the church. I met with Elder Cunningham at 2:15 pm at a local restaurant. He told me Bishop Turner reached out to him to be the liaison between him and me.

Bishop Turner had four requests:
- Give him a chance to apologize and ask for forgiveness
- He would compensate me for my pain and suffering
- He would resign from his position if it were necessary

☐ Lastly, to sign a statement withdrawing my complaint against him and the Zion Apostolic Church.

Elder Cunningham stressed the severity of this matter. It was greater than we knew and they pretended to be concerned about the people of God. He said they had lost me and did not want to lose any more members. Imagine that! Now our brother the Lord was concerned about the one, even when 99 went astray. He DID go after the one that was lost.

Cunningham said they would correct this situation as soon as possible. I told him it sounded like a bribe and I refused to be a part of another cover-up. I also told him this type of sexual immorality had been going on since the early 50's, and the Lord did not give me courage to expose this illness to turn around and put another Band-Aid on it. Cunningham kept stressing the need for an answer by Friday. I wondered why there was such a rush for me to talk to Turner by Friday. Frustrated from his ridiculous pleads, I resolved to get back to him. I just wanted him out of my presence. How dare he not make me matter. It was about me. The only concern for these supposed man of cloth was to save their backs, the church name, and me, looking like a fool and a liar.

Well, I left there feeling angry because my spirit was not agreeing with any of this. I called Elder Snipes and Elder Ballard; we did a three-way conference call. I told them what transpired in the meeting at the restaurant. Elders

Snipes and Ballard were appalled. We agreed that we would continue to move forward to investigate this matter. This was out of my hands. It's now in the hands of God.

Elder Cunningham called me the next day, but I did not answer. He called repeatedly and left messages saying I need to call in. It was absolutely urgent that I speak with him that day. I ignored the messages. In fact, I saved them for documentation. In his persistence to ring my phone, I answered letting him know I was not ready to meet with Turner nor comfortable with the request by Turner. Cunningham had the mitigated gall to say I was not a part of Zion Apostolic anymore, but he was. They were trying to save Zion Apostolic and needed my help to save face. They were desperate and begging me to cooperate. He said the brethren who received those letters need healing and we need to end this and that I am the only one who can do this. I continued to say NO. He asked if I would at least consider signing the statement to withdraw my complaint. He was really stressing me out with all the pressure. I'm not usually rude with people, but I was being pushed to that point. I told him I was through discussing the matter and hung up.

Elder Winfrey called me later that evening to say my letter was not being ignored and I would be getting an official letter from the investigating committee. He wanted to know what I wanted done and if I would speak with Bishop Turner. I told him no, and hung up. It angered me that he was appointed to investigate this matter while he misused his authority. He took advantage of me. I was not aware a meeting was scheduled with the investigating committee the next day at the headquarters church.

The elders named in the letter were questioned in this meeting. Elder Terrell denied the accusations. Elder Yandle confessed his part of the allegations to talk inappropriately about his body parts. Turner denied my allegations. Elder Weston, who pastors the church in Lenexa, KS, read my letter to the committee and I was told one of the Elders abruptly left the meeting. Minister Woodard followed him to a pawnshop where he was seen trying to purchase a gun. It was then I understood the urgency of Cunningham wanting me to sign that statement. They were planning to pay me $100,000.00 under the table, and wave the signed statement in the faces of the investigating committee and say, "I told you she was a liar!" but it backfired in their faces.

ViNita Williams Davis

THE BETRAYAL OF FAMILY & FRIENDS
Chapter Ten

"When we suffer, let us remember that God will bring comfort to us through His Word, by the Holy Spirit and through fellow believers. God does not comfort us so that we'll be comfortable; we are comforted by God so that we can be comforters to others."
II Corinthians 1:3-11

You Are My Strength
William Murphy

Elder and Sister Ballard along with Elder Sanders who was an associate Minister at Emporia headquarters, agreed to accompany me to my parents' home to speak with them about what I was going through. It was time for me to inform them because the word was getting out and I wanted them to hear it from me and not the church gossip. I was afraid to go by myself; I needed support of the Elders. I was very disappointed with my dad's reaction. He wanted me to forgive Bishop Turner and go on with my life because people are human and they make mistakes. The elders tried to explain to him that a wrong had been done and that it should be handled by the elders. My dad did not want this to go public; he wanted it to be handled by the elders in a dignified manner. My dad made it clear that I should not take any money that was offered to me. He said I should just drop it. I left in tears and very hurt by his attitude of defending his pastor instead of his daughter. I left feeling defeated. I did not want to hurt my family.

I got myself together a few days later with the determination to continue seeking justice. Elder Weston scheduled a meeting with the investigating committee at the sister church in Westwood, KS where Elder Wilson pastored. Those present were Elders Snipes, Wilson, Gilmore, Sumter, Weston, along with Michelle, Essie and my mom. We were informed that Elder Cunningham was in Elder Wilson's office. Elder Weston had his tape recorder to take minutes, and Elder Ballad and I had our tape recorders for our personal documentation.

The meeting began with me reading a statement. Elder Wilson said he was sorry for what I went through. Elder Snipes asked the committee what my accusers had to say. They would not answer that question. Wilson and Weston kept excusing themselves to speak with Cunningham, who was in Wilson's office. They seemed to be getting permission to answer questions. When they returned to the meeting, in frustration Snipes and Sanders wanted all to know the meeting was being manipulated by Turner who was dictating the meeting by phone to Cunningham. This is when Sister Michelle spoke up and said, "If they are going to railroad my sister, I will get me an attorney and go to court to say that Bishop Turner did the same thing to me." Everyone was shocked; no one was expecting this testimony. It was all on tape and in my mind, that's all we needed, for someone else to come forward.

The meeting was adjourned because of the manipulation between Turner and Cunningham.

A few months later, it was rumored that a certain woman was silenced with a payoff of $50,000 to recant her story, but it wasn't me, it wasn't my Mom and it wasn't Sister Essie.

Several weeks later Elder and Sister Ballad came up from Newton. We had an appointment with an attorney and thought Michelle would go with us. We called her but she told Elder Ballad that happened years ago and she had forgiven Turner for his actions. She recanted her statement, but forgot we had it on tape. I was hurt about her changing her mind. We were beginning to bond as sisters-in-Christ. This crushed my trust in everyone. The so-called friends I had at Zion Apostolic turned their backs on me once the truth was out about the deceit and cover-ups in this organization.

Sister Belinda had been a member for about 3 years. She shared that she was already in civil litigations for sexual molestation against her former pastor, who once attended Zion Apostolic as a youth. She spoke to her attorney about my case and her attorney agreed to meet with me after the closing her case. She went through this from a teenager to her early 20's. She also said her former pastor did the same thing to several younger sisters in his church. Belinda left that organization because of the lawsuit. She left with many members upset with her because she had exposed her pastor. She spoke with her attorney about taking my case and she did.

I met with Attorney Margaret Lyles the next day. Belinda met me after she got off from work to introduce me to her. While talking with Attorney Lyles, I was so broken I cried the entire time. She agreed to take my case and allowed me to make installment payments on her retainer. When I left her office, I felt so relieved and I'd finally found someone to take my case. I even volunteered my office skills and helped her organize files in her office.

In the meantime, my sister Marie and parents were still on my back about dropping the case with the church. I stopped going by as often because every time I would visit, I left in tears. I did not want to burden them with my decision to continue with the case.

Elder Weston called to say a meeting would be held the next day at the headquarters church and I should come to make a statement to the ministerial body. It was very cloudy that evening, a storm was coming and I was getting anxious about getting home before the rain.

The meeting began at 7:00 pm. Twenty minutes into the meeting; they had not called me in. This was a stalling tactic. Therefore, I made my entrance into the meeting. Elder Cunningham told me I could not come in. I turned to him with my hand facing him, and said, "I know you are not talking to me." At that time, Bishop Turner rushed out of the meeting. I said, "Go ahead and call the police so I can let them know what is going on." Elder Weston gently guided me out and asked me to give them ten more minutes. I waited in the hall with Deacon Perry and Chief Deacon Randall. They were very kind and gentle with me as we talked in the hallway.

While standing there, a police officer approached us and asked if there was a problem. Chief Randal said no there was not a problem, everything was under control. The officer left and we continued talking. I left because I realized they weren't going to let me make a statement.

Because of my irate state, my friend Sister Essie drove me home. Considering the storm I had just left with these fake men of the cloth, she was compassionate enough to be there for me. She knew that because of my impaired vision, I didn't need the added stress of the rain.

Elder Ballad & Snipes came by after the short meeting. They said Bishop Turner came back in the meeting and yelled at everyone, saying he was not going to allow anyone to come in a meeting uninvited. Elder Leroy Wiggins took a stand and told Bishop that he was not going to talk down to the ministers in that manner, and that they deserved to hear what I had to say. Bishop Turner said the meeting was over, he turned the lights out and left the elders in the dark.

The ministerial body was very upset to know Bishop Turner called the police to remove me from the church grounds. Many pastors had traveled from Florida, Georgia, and North Carolina for this meeting to be disrespected by their leader.

Before I went to bed, I wrote this letter and sent it via email to the pastors who attended the meeting.

I would like to say that I am sorry for my outburst on last night. I only wanted to make a statement and leave. I wanted these brethren to look me in my eyes and tell me I was lying. I wanted to assure them that no one had influenced me. Also, when I broke my silence, several men of God asked me not to do anything, just allow the Elders to handle this. I listened to this for three weeks and decided to write the letter.

This is NOT about money. I DO NOT want their dirty money. Bishop Turner sent Elder Cunningham to offer me a settlement of $100, 000.00 for my pain and suffering, if I would agree to sign a statement withdrawing my complaint. I said NO, I would not be a part of a cover up. I am only trying to protect other sisters from these ungodly men.

ViNita Williams Davis

I wanted to remind Elder Yandle that he has a daughter the same age as his victims. I wanted to say to him, if he can preach all over his sins to my Mother and sister, God help him. I wanted to ask Bishop Turner how he could even look at my parents in their eyes.

In closing, I want to say that I am through with this and I am going on with my life. I am giving these men over to the Lord. The Lord sees what is going on in this church with the leadership. This is not my fight. This one belongs to God! This is His battle, He is going to shake the foundation of this organization, and the walls will come down.

Attorney Allan received word about the police being called and he was not pleased with the decision to call in law enforcement.

> *Dear Brethren:*
> *I have just returned from a trial here in Philadelphia and received notice that the finding of the Review Committee has been circulated. I also have learned of a most disturbing occurrence at the Home Church in Emporia, where the police was actually summoned by someone when Sister Baily appeared and attempted to make a presentation to the ministerial body. Whatever the reason for this solicitation of law enforcement officers, I write to announce my strong disapproval of such efforts being undertaken by anyone.*
>
> *Matters of this nature, especially among clergy, should be handled within the church, if possible. From the information*

provided to me, I have concluded that the decision to solicit the police and/or law enforcement to attempt to remove Sister Bailey from the premises was inappropriate and ill advised. Even if she was not granted the privilege of addressing the body, I am confident that the Spirit of Christ, rather than the law enforcement personnel, would have been sufficient to maintain order.

Moreover, throughout the review process, I have been provided information regarding some of the allegations registered against various ministers and senior leaders of the church. As a member of the clergy, I have suggested that all allegations of wrongdoing should be investigated, irrespective of the initial scope of the Review Committee's charge.

The Elders are duty-bound to investigate wrongdoing among the clergy. Given the fact that apparently at least one other sister has come forward suggesting that similar misbehavior was perpetrated against her by a senior member of the clergy, it would be unreasonable and inappropriate for such additional allegations not to be investigated. The clergy must be blameless and beyond reproach in order to be effective ambassadors for Christ. Accordingly, if there is any effort undertaken to silence these other accusers and/or not to investigate their charges, let it go on record now to make clear that I did not approve and/or agree with such efforts. The charges must be investigated and appropriate vindications and/or discipline dispensed.

One of the brethren called me to inquire whether I was providing legal representation to any party involved in the investigation. I have not. While I am a lawyer in the state of

ViNita Williams Davis

Philadelphia, I am not licensed to practice law in Kansas. Thus, I cannot and have not represented anyone, accused or accuser, relating in any way to any matters being reviewed by the church. While only one brother approached me regarding this issue, I write to all to make clear that my role has simply been that of a concerned member of the beloved Zion Apostolic Church and minister of the Gospel.

Finally, this present exercise/investigation demonstrates to me the need for administrative controls to be put in place for the orderly conduct of the Zion Apostolic organization. There needs to be board of Bishops and other designated authority figures, as prescribed by the church constitution and bylaws, so that appropriate accountability can be maintained. Jesus' selection of eleven faithful apostles is a good example to follow.

Yours in Christ,

Attorney T. Allan

I thank and praise God for Attorney Allan for being instrumental in advising the elders on how to handle this case. He is a no nonsense minister and attorney who possess integrity. I'm sure when he witnessed to me in 1980; it was not for me to be subjected to the turmoil and harassment I endured at Zion Apostolic. I also thank God for his sister Rene'. When other so-called friends turned their backs on me, she stepped in and encouraged me through the entire process. She, like her brother, stood for the truth. Lies and deceit are not an option in her life. Rene' was always concerned about my safety when it came to Bishop Turner and his sons. She often told me to watch my surroundings because the devil was on a rampage. She was fearful that they would try to get revenge. God is good; He protected me through the entire ordeal.

LETTING GO AND MOVING FORWARD
Chapter Eleven

"Brethren, I count not myself to have apprehended: but this one thing I do, forgetting those things which are behind, and reaching forth unto those things which are before, I press toward the mark for the prize of the high calling of God in Christ Jesus."
Philippians 3: 13-14

"Let Go, Let God"
Dewayne Woods

During this time, my Mother was diagnosed with stage four-colon cancer. I found out that Bishop Turner called my elderly parents to his office to try to get them to encourage me to drop my lawsuit. He shared with them the letter that I wrote to him and the elders. He convinced my parents that Elder Ballad was influencing me to file a lawsuit. That was SO not true. I filed the suit because I was not able to get justice from church leaders.

My Mother was grieved by Bishop Turner dumping these lies on her. He had no compassion for the people of God. He did whatever he could to turn the light off him. A couple of weeks later, both Bishop Turner and I had our depositions taken in Attorney Lyles office. While we were being deposed, I could not look at him; just to see his face and be in his presence caused me to go through mental stress. He lied on so many questions that were asked of him. I could not believe what I was hearing. His attorney I. J. Lemon said to me "Your parents don't even believe you." I replied, "Yea Right, keep on thinking that." We spent about three hours in the deposition. I was so relieved when it was over so I could leave thier presence.

A month later, about 30 elders were subpoenaed to testify on my behalf. For two and half hours, my attorney kept me in her office interrogating me on what the true elders would say on my behalf. I didn't know for sure, but I knew that their integrity would speak volumes. She kept badgering me why I thought we could win this case. It had been two years since she had my case, and now she ask all of these questions? I was feeling so frustrated. She had several conversations with Elder Snipes from Florida and Elder Ballard about those raising funds to assist me in paying her fees. This frustrated her to the point that she asked me, "They don't know anything about not leaving a paper trail?" I thought to myself, this doesn't sound or feel right. I heard that she had been suspended by the Bar about 20 years ago. I did not know the reason, and I just trusted she would do the right thing. Elder Ballad mailed me $500.00 from his personal funds to give her on that day, but she would not accept it. She would always refer to the elders as being full of "rhetoric."

Finally I gave up. I through my hands up and said, "Just drop the case." She asked me why I was dropping the case. I could not believe this woman! She said the church attorneys would be willing to drop the "defamation of character counter suit if I was willing to drop my case. That statement let me know that the meeting was to apply pressure on me to drop the case. I just cried. I felt so defeated. When I left her office, I called the college to speak with Dean McNeil and Professor Larson. Because I was so distraught, I needed them to pray for me. I was afraid to go home. The suicidal ideation was beginning to overwhelm me. They called to check on me later that night. I made it through the night, by the grace of God. The next day I called the mental health facility and told my doctor what happened and that I needed to be admitted because I did not trust the devil with the thoughts that I was having. I stayed there for about a week and I was released. My thought pattern was better, and now I had to focus on my dying mother and try to move on with my life.

It has been six years since I dropped the case, and I am still waiting for a bill from my attorney on the balance. Just like she said about the paper trail, I don't have a balance because she knows how to deal under the table. Yes, Bishop Turner and his team paid her off.

My family and I spent the last Mother's Day at the

hospital showering our mother with love. She was somewhat alert at times, but sleeping most of the time because of the medication to keep her comfortable. Two days before she made her transition, I got close to her and whispered in her ear, I dropped the case. It was then that she opened her eyes and she assured me by saying, "Praise God honey, don't worry about it, this was not your battle, it's the Lord's. He is going to take care of the injustice that you and many other sisters have gone through." Oh how my heart rejoiced to know she believed me. I made a statement at her home going service that she was my silent prayer partner. She had knowledge of several sisters in her local church who had been sexual harassed by their pastor. She was a prayer warrior. She was a quiet and humble woman of God. I made the statement because I wanted Bishop Turner and his attorney to know that my mother went to her grave believing me.

After the service, while everyone was greeting the family, my sister-in-law informed me that Bishop Turner's wife (First Lady) made a remark to her saying; she doesn't know why I made remarks about my mother, because I am the one who killed her. When I got home, I emailed Bishop Turner to inform him about the remark his wife made. I told him he needed to get his wife in check before I do, because her comments were awful coming from a First Lady and if she knew anything about the Bible, it says that we all have an appointed time to die, and this was an appointment that my mom could not cancel. She was ready to meet her Savior.

I began to let go of the past and negative emotions associated with my past hurt, disappointment, fear, shame, and regret. I now realize these negative emotions were too heavy to carry. They weighted me down and darkened my spirit.

RECOVERY: THE WOUNDS AND THE SCARS
Chapter Twelve

"The spirit of a man will sustain his infirmity; but a wounded spirit who can bear?"
Proverbs 18:14

For I know the thoughts that I think towards you, saith the Lord, thoughts of peace, and not of evil, to give you an expected end.
Jeremiah 29:11

"There's A Healing"
Donald Lawrence

Going through the journey of recovery, I see life more clearly. I am growing stronger each day. As far as my mental health, I continue my counseling sessions and see my Psychiatrist every month. I recall the times when I was not taking my meds as ordered because I knew they would not fix my problem. Yet I would self-medicate with pain pills hoping to take away the emotional pain that I was experiencing. I refused to talk about the inner turmoil that was slowly killing me because I was so ashamed for not knowing how to defend myself.

For a year, I entered a program at the area mental health

called Dialectical Behavior Therapy. It was a very intense program requiring lots of discipline. Many times I wanted to quit, but I kept pushing to make it through because I wanted to get better. In this program, I learned survival skills like how to control my thought pattern, how to stand up for my rights, how to say NO, and feel good about myself. During this time, I could see myself becoming empowered with those skills that I formerly lacked. My self-esteem was so low and I was full of self-hate. The thoughts of death often consumed my mind. I was obsessed with dying at an early age. I began making funeral plans at the age of 28, shortly after my divorce with Mel. Every year I would go back and revise the program outline. When so-called friends abandoned me, I removed their names from the program. I often believed because I had diabetes, the complications of the disease would be my demise before 40.

After turning 40, I continued to be obsessed with this enemy called death. I could not believe I actually made it to the big Four O. I was still dealing with the struggle of sexual harassment from church brethren and suicide, but God kept me from myself. I gave a testimony recently at my church about depression and suicidal ideations. I told them I was consumed with dying and now I can truly say, "I ain't got time to die because I have found the purpose in which God has for me.

My spiritual growth certainly progressed through the years. As I look back on the years I lost at Zion

Apostolic with so many distractions, I will continue praising and thanking God for not giving up on me, and for not allowing the enemy to destroy me. I often think about the many sisters who were sexually harassed, left Zion Apostolic, and no longer attend anybody's church. So many people have been hurt and damaged through this organization. I get comfort in knowing God will hold these men responsible for scattering His sheep. I am so thankful to God for giving me the strength and courage to expose this ungodly behavior and to leave this organization.

I often have sisters from Zion Apostolic call and ask me if I was being truthful about my allegations against Bishop Turner, and my response to them is, "I have a fear of God and I would never lie on a man of God." They are now beginning to see things and question the rumors that have been traveling among the congregation since I left. There were times when it bothered me to see the members continue to sit under such corrupt leadership. I never expected the elderly to get up and leave, but I certainly was disappointed in the middle-aged generation who said they believed me, while the other half turned their backs on me. The young adults certainly lost the respect they once held for the leadership.

ViNita Williams Davis

EPILOGUE
The Victory

———◆———

For his anger endureth but a moment; in his favour is life: weeping may endure for a night, but joy commeth in the morning.
Psalms 30:5

"God Favored Me"
Hezekiah Walker

Because of glaucoma and low vision, I had to make a decision about my night driving and the distance I was traveling to church. It was becoming very dangerous. I thank God for my son who prevented me from getting into many accidents while traveling from church. I prayed about whether I should transfer my membership to a closer church. I have never been the one to church-hop. It has been seven years since I left Zion Apostolic and joined my new church with Bishop Barry Scott. I had grown spiritually under his leadership. I thank God for the saints and the man of God who preached the Word of God and bought life back into this broken vessel of mine.

I spoke with Pastor Scott concerning my health challenges and low vision. I asked if he would allow me to transfer to one of the sister churches we fellowship with, 10 minutes from my home. He was sad to see me leave, but he understood my health challenges and granted me the transfer. He called Bishop Lowery to set up a meeting to speak with him concerning me transferring. It's ironic how life comes full circle. I was baptized in Jesus Name at Round Top United church in the late 70's by Bishop Lowery, and now I'm back home where I should have stayed. I often wonder how my life would have turned out if only I had remained at Round-Top, but that doesn't matter because I'm back now and enjoying Jesus and my new church family. I thank and praise God for my pastor, First Lady, and new friends. My Pastor is very knowledgeable of the Word and it shows in his preaching and teaching. He is a true man of God who has the people of God in his heart.

I will not promote my pain or feel sorry for myself. No matter how deep my wounds, they carry with them great lessons. My wounds have given me the patience to endure, the maturity to grow, the compassion to reach out to others in need, the courage to survive, the character to transform something hurtful into something positive, and the faith to know that I am not alone.

It is sometimes difficult to thank God for our struggles and pain. When we trust God through the easy and the difficult times we grow close to Him. The closer we draw to Him, the easier it is to thank Him for all things. Thankfulness keeps us focused on the positive. It reminds us that there is always hope, and that the difficulties will pass. Wounds have their limits, but thankfulness doesn't. I have learned through my struggles that the greater my gratitude, the more I become aware of my healing. Jesus is truly the ultimate physician.

Journeying through times of trouble, two things in particular that I thank God for. First, I am thankful for the wounds themselves, and my faithfulness to endure. In the end, I will always know that God loves me and that He is there to heal my wounds when the time is right. He has strengthened me because I learned to trust and believe His word.

He is my strength! He lightened my darkness, and for the first time in my life, I can say that I am in peace, surrounded by His love and mercy. He shielded me with his faithfulness, and for that, I am eternally grateful.

I am standing on His promise. He will never leave nor forsake me. I am holding on to His joy, peace, purpose, and especially His hope. It is through hope I can move forward and in moving forward, I know God will meet my every need.

I want to say thank you to all of my so-called friends who turned their backs on me when I needed them the most. Thank you for creating space for the Lord to replace you with genuine loving friends.

Thanks to the pastors who wanted me to have due process so, the wrong could be corrected.

Thank you Lord for preparing a table before my enemies, but not allowing them to destroy me.

Most importantly, thank you Lord for restoring the joy and peace that I lost. Thank you for allowing me to pass this lesson and never to repeat it again. Thank you for increasing my faith in You. Thank you for giving me the boldness to stand tall and never be afraid.

I know that I can do nothing without God's favor and grace.

Be patient and wait expectantly for God. He does things in His own time, no matter how long we have to wait. He has given us this hope that is an anchor for the soul, firm and secure. He is worth the wait!

And now I pronounce benediction over my past hurts, and for the people who I allowed to afflict pain in my life. I am no more a victim but victorious in Christ Jesus. It is all over and I forgive you.

SCRIPTURES

Now unto him that is able to do exceeding abundantly above all that we ask or think, according to the power that worketh in us, Unto him be glory in the church by Christ Jesus throughout all ages, world without end. Amen."
Ephesians 3:10-21

"And now shall mine head be lifted up above mine enemies round about me: therefore will I offer in his tabernacle sacrifices of joy; I will sing, yea, I will sing praises unto the LORD." Psalm 27:6

"The Windows of Heaven Are Opened"
Author unknown

The windows of heaven are open
The blessings are falling tonight
There's joy, joy, joy in my heart
For Jesus made everything right
I gave Him my old tattered garments
He gave me a robe of pure white
Now I'm feasting on manna from heaven
And that's why I'm happy tonight

ViNita Williams Davis

Thank you Pastor Schneider for sharing such a powerful testimony that seals my story as a witness of how the LORD can bless us with VICTORY and not ever be victimized again.

ViNita, after reading the manuscript about your life and the many crises that pushed you into writing this book, I extend to you heartfelt thanks.

As humans, we all are subject to test and trials, which is a part of our development and growth. Some experiences we may count as good, while others appear to not be so good, but they are still designed to all work out for our good. My first encounter with you was around 1981 when I met you, your mom, and sister. As a member of Zion Apostolic Church, my family was greatly involved, with my then husband Eugene becoming the assistant pastor. Although there were early signs of concerns, looking back, we were blind. Eugene was a very prestigious Community Insurance Executive, which in the eyes of Pastor Yandle and his wife, along with the home church leadership, viewed us as wealthy. We were the subjects of notoriety. Often times, large sums of money were given to the leadership, to meet their wants as our three children and myself were denied the necessary needs. Our daughter Ann, at around age 11, shared with her father and I that God had spoken to her to tell us to leave that church. as it was not for our family, and in essence much harm would come to our family, if we didn't leave. We took her prophetic words as a childish voice, only to later realize, God truly did speak through her to help us. We choose not to listen.

Eugene, a college graduate, was being sucked into their scheme of control and manipulation. His role was changing into verbal and physical abusive actions that divided our once peaceful home. Vacations became a nightmare with the Pastor Yandle and his wife taking our vacation time as theirs. They would travel with us, four adults in a car, along with three children. As the years rolled by, we were becoming less of family, and being pulled into deception and control.

The doctrinal teaching was generally one of confusion and some sexual discourses that always had some interpretation that validated the Scriptures with the intent to justify the need for living "holy." One never measured up to the teachings. Confessions of sins were openly voiced before the whole congregation, which was being taught throughout the whole Zion Apostolic organization. Numerous acts of sexual encounters among leaders and members were a reality. The judgment sentence was harsh for sisters, while the brothers were unscathed.

Eugene became a spiritual spy, reporting to Pastor Yandle our every move, or he was asked to stand in collaboration with some unscriptural stance that often left the victim feeling embarrassed or ashamed.

ViNita, by this time you had left the church, but was granted permission to change membership to the home church, and our paths only crossed during the larger gatherings. I often saw you dealing with issues, which I did not fully understand.

Having the gift of discernment, I saw much and heard a lot, but for fear of rebuttal and being caught, I had little conversations about what the Holy Spirit was saying or showing me. Your mom and I talked...she too saw and heard a lot.

When we could no longer handle the spiritual and physical attacks toward the children, after much deliberation in prayer, I too left, but never to go to another Zion Apostolic organization church. I took our three children and left. On the night of my deliverance, Eugene stood and told the pastor and people I was going through a mental battle, and he knew nothing of my plans, which appeared to make me look crazy. Strangely, the whole church appeared shocked, as I was then labeled as infidel along with our children. Life at home became unbearable. Pastor Yandle along with the Presiding Bishop, made our lives miserable, by shunning us. ViNita this is only a small part of the many emotional abuses that occurred.

Thank you for opening up the truth, as for Eugene he remained, we later divorced, and since 2011, he has been in a VA Health Care facility. In 2015, he sent word through our daughter, that he needed to talk with me. After much prayer, I called him and most of the abusive treatment toward me and the children had gone. He acknowledged, that Pastor Yandle and the leaders along with many remembered situations they were scripturally wrong, abusing their authority and power. He also acknowledged the confessions of young girls molested, sexual exploits among leadership and members, mishandling of money. Now, 2015, Pastor Yandle takes members insurance policies, and makes himself the beneficiary or becomes the power of attorney over member's personal savings, checking and IRA's and credit cards. This is evident that he is also a thief, taking out large sums of money for personal gain, and writing out checks for his wife and children. My heart goes out to the innocent victims who have, and still are being hurt by the leadership of Zion Apostolic Church.

Please be encouraged. God has directed you to write the truth, which is a part of the puzzle that I hope will set others free from bondage. Your book is open, may those who read this find healing and deliverance and true spiritual freedom.

Pastor Ann Schneider
Girard, Ohio

REVIEW

ViNita and I have been friends for more than 60 years. While our friendship has remained strong, my friend, sister and beloved classmate has had to deal with a rocky road. I was elated when she asked me to read and review Wounded in the House of God with the Audacity to Survive "Silence is no Longer an Option"; however, reading her dreadful unawakening ordeal opened my eyes as to why ViNita, for most of her life, most always displayed a depressed state of mind. I often wondered why and who caused her to fall into this slumbered mood. Her journey as a wounded woman being molested as a child, staying in an abusive marriage, sexual harassment both in the work place and church has given me a new perspective on why her disposition seemed so low most of the time.

Reading and digesting the documentation of her life has proven more than challenging for me. One would not think a person with a golden heart has prevailed in spite of all the many rejections, abuse, and health challenges she has endured. Even in her pain and struggles to survive, she continues to press her way to a higher calling in Christ, life and relationships with trusted friends. As she indicated in her book, most of the time she used pain medication to help ease her mental pain. Our Lord, and Savior Jesus Christ, kept her through the years, when even she wanted to take her own life. As much as I could, with as little information I had, I tried to embrace and encourage her to move in the right direction. I knew Nita, as I affectionately call her, needed comfort and the words from those who loved her and expected nothing of her. She gave the best and should expect the best. Her willingness to give and help others through life caused her to become a silent keeper of horrible things that caused mental health problems.

As is documented throughout her book, she relied heavily on her spiritual wellbeing to carry her through. While I did not say this to her, my thoughts were always that the organization (place of worship) she considered her sanctuary was destroying her mentally and physically. I suspected that Nita was challenged by something in her life but did not know what. Her silence kept her mental status in shambles for years. Nita has had more than her fair share of obstacles, but she has also had a will to survive. Her healing has just begun.

When your enemy wants you to go away, God gives you the strength and courage to move forward with victory even if things don't seem to be going your way. This is when one who believes and trusts will understand that God has his own plan and for her to have the audacity to survive, declare victory, and live, shows "silence is no longer an option." Remaining silent was her worst flaw.

My respect and love for her is deep and it really saddens me that she was taken advantage of for most of her life. While this book is well documented of past hurts, it will be up to Nita to let God continue to guide her in the right direction.

Life is a journey that only God can guide. Let no man set this course for you. Love is where the heart is. Let no man destroy it. Silence is never golden when your mental state of mind causes you to wonder.

Respectfully,
Phyllis Lewis Thompson, Childhood friend & Classmate

Having read my aunt's story and piecing it together with little I knew of her struggles with depression, it makes sense in a shocking and disappointing manner. As I read her experience, abuse, pain, betrayal, fears, and risk, I'm empowered and inspired by her strength to remain standing. I'm convinced ever more of God's love, protection, mercy and His promises to His children.

I'm enlightened by my Grandmother's consistent wisdom that she has instilled in our family that God will fight our battles and see us through. My aunt's story reigns and resonate the raw truth that all individuals can somehow relate to in any situation in life. It's a testimony, especially in this day and time, that although the devil works through the unexpected, God sits high and looks low and He will pull the covers off the unrighteousness and will restore the righteous if we keep our faith in Him.

Her journey is also a reminder to the saints of God that we must always keep our eyes on God as our Lord and Savior and never put our trust in man to save us nor condemn us to hell; but only to reverence the true men of God as servants and messengers of Christ. I'm more than grateful for my aunt Nita's courage and willingness to live out her purpose for Christ to "cry loud and spare not", trusting that more souls will be saved and healed through her message of God's redemption, restoration and omnipotent love!

Princess Williams, Niece

ViNita Williams Davis

ABOUT THE AUTHOR

―――――◆―――――

ViNita Williams Davis – 1953 was born in Columbia, S.C.

She is affectionately called "Nita" to those closest to her. She has an eclectic appetite for many schools of learning. A 1971 graduate of C.A. Johnson High School, a 1981 graduate from Rice College with a certification in medical office administration. She matriculated to Kenneth Shuler School of Cosmetology and graduated in 1991. Moreover in 2013, she earned a Master's Degree in Christian Ministry from Central Christian University. ViNita retired in 2005 from Palmetto Richland Hospital with twenty-five years of service as a Unit Secretary in the Neonatal Intensive Care Unit.

In her Christian walk with Christ, Nita was baptized in Jesus name and filled with the precious gift of the Holy Spirit.

Ms. Davis has accomplished much in her life; academics and her two beautiful children. Currently she is the President of the C.A. Johnson Class of '71, Vice President of the C.A. Johnson Alumni Association, the former President of the South Carolina Diabetes Coalition, and serves as a member of the South Carolina Diabetes Today Advisory Council. She mentors women inmates at Alvin S.

Glenn Detention Center, and sits presently on the boards of directors at Central Christian University of South Carolina and the Pen of a Ready Writer Society.

ViNita enjoys Desk Top Publishing, designing and building web sites. Planning programs and events are her passion. She draws strength from doing acts of kindness to encourage those who are sometimes over looked and treated indifferently. Her enthusiasm for her Salvation, her willingness to pay the price for her integrity, and ministering to those who are hurting, is her purpose in life.

www.ingramcontent.com/pod-product-compliance
Lightning Source LLC
Chambersburg PA
CBHW051954290426
44110CB00015B/2231